Cambridge Elements

Elements in Religion and Monotheism
edited by
Paul K. Moser
Loyola University Chicago
Chad Meister
Bethel University

HINDU MONOTHEISM

Gavin Flood
Oxford University

CAMBRIDGE
UNIVERSITY PRESS

CAMBRIDGE
UNIVERSITY PRESS

University Printing House, Cambridge CB2 8BS, United Kingdom

One Liberty Plaza, 20th Floor, New York, NY 10006, USA

477 Williamstown Road, Port Melbourne, VIC 3207, Australia

314–321, 3rd Floor, Plot 3, Splendor Forum, Jasola District Centre, New Delhi – 110025, India

79 Anson Road, #06–04/06, Singapore 079906

Cambridge University Press is part of the University of Cambridge.

It furthers the University's mission by disseminating knowledge in the pursuit of education, learning, and research at the highest international levels of excellence.

www.cambridge.org
Information on this title: www.cambridge.org/9781108731140
DOI: 10.1017/9781108584289

First published 2020

A catalogue record for this publication is available from the British Library.

ISBN 978-1-108-73114-0 Paperback
ISSN 2631-3014 (online)
ISSN 2631-3006 (print)

Hindu Monotheism

Elements in Religion and Monotheism

DOI: 10.1017/9781108584289
First published online: August 2020

Gavin Flood
Oxford University

Author for correspondence: Gavin Flood, gavin.flood@theology.ox.ac.uk

Abstract: If by monotheism we mean the idea of a single transcendent God who creates the universe out of nothing (*creatio ex nihilo*), as in the Abrahamic religions, then that is not found in the history of Hinduism. But if we mean a supreme, transcendent deity who impels the universe, sustains it, and ultimately destroys it before causing it to emerge once again, who is the ultimate source of all other gods who are her or his emanations, then this idea does develop within that history. It is a Hindu monotheism and its nature that is the topic of this Element.

Keywords: Hinduism, Shiva, Vishnu, *Bhagavad-gītā*

ISBNs: 9781108731140 (PB), 9781108584289 (OC)
ISSNs: 2631-3014 (online), 2631-3006 (print)

Contents

Introduction

A Reflection on Hindu Theology

Hindu monotheism may at first sound like an oxymoron. One thing that seems to characterize Hinduism is its plurality of gods. Yet many Hindus will claim that this plurality expresses a single deity, that all the gods are aspects of one power as iconographically depicted in the image of Kṛṣṇa's universal form (*viśvarūpa*) from chapter 11 of the *Bhagavad-gītā*, where he reveals his singular nature with pluriform aspects to the hero Arjuna. This element describes the emergence of the idea of a single deity being the source of all the others and of the universe itself. It charts the rise of theism – and specifically the idea of monotheism – in the history of Hindu traditions through textual sources.

As the example of Kṛṣṇa's universal form demonstrates, there was a monotheism before the influence of Islam or Christianity, and this Element describes this development in the history of traditions that have become known as Hinduism. Hinduism comprises a complex set of traditions that share cultural forms and patterns. The word itself is of recent origin, coming to prominence in the nineteenth century and the word 'Hindu' not being used before the sixteenth century, when it distinguished one group of people from Muslims or Yavanas in Bengal and Kashmir (O'Connell 2019: 188–96). But it is legitimate to use the word anachronistically because the traditions that it comes to denote have their origin in ancient texts regarded as revelation, the Veda, and we can trace a continuity of historical forms through to the present. There are unifying tendencies within Hindu traditions (Nicholson 2010), although the relationship between the category Hinduism and traditions such as Śaiva or Vaiṣṇava is complex (see, for example, Fisher 2017: 5–14). It is also important to note that Hinduism is defined less by belief than by practice. As Frits Staal observed long ago, it is not what a Hindu believes that is definitional but what he or she does (Staal 1989: 389). Hinduism is arguably more of an orthopraxy than an orthodoxy, identified by what Michaels calls an identificatory habitus that regulates, ritually, most aspects of life (Michaels 2016: 3). If there is a thesis in this Element, it is that Hindu monotheism is intimately linked to history, to social and political developments of Indic civilization such as the rise of kingship, but that the philosophical and theological discourse that articulates it cannot be simply reduced to political and sociological factors: we can examine Hindu monotheism as the history of an idea textually instantiated.

This Element predominantly describes and traces the history of an idea, but it also offers some theological reflection. If God is outside of the universe, can he or she be known? Is there anything positive to be said about God or can God only be approached through the negation of all attributes? And so on. The topic of Hindu monotheism has been addressed by others, in particular the pioneering works of Nicol Macnicol's *Indian Theism* (1915) and Gopikamohan Bhattacharya's *Studies in Nyāya-Vaiśeṣika Theism* (1961), and has also been addressed by Julius Lipner (1978, 2017) among others. This study is a modest contribution to the theme. The predominant language of Hindu scriptures is Sanskrit, but Tamil scriptures are also important and vernacular languages – both Indo-Aryan and Dravidian – come to play increasingly important roles in the development of the traditions.[1]

If by monotheism we mean the idea of a single transcendent God who creates the universe out of nothing (*creatio ex nihilo*), as in the Abrahamic religions, then it is open to question whether or not that idea is found in the history of Hinduism. But if we mean a supreme, transcendent deity who impels the universe (whether created from nothing or not), sustains it, and ultimately destroys it before causing it to emerge once again, who is the ultimate source of all other gods who are her or his emanations, then this idea does develop within that history. The purpose of this Element is therefore not to seek for a monotheism that approximates to the Abrahamic model, with its implicit assumption of an evolution towards that ideal, but rather to use the category as a lens through which to understand important developments within the history of Hinduism in which a single, transcendent deity comes to dominate theological discourse, whose nature is the subject of much intellectual debate, which becomes the focus of devotion, and which attracts royal patronage. It is a *Hindu* monotheism and its nature that is the topic of this Element.

This is not intended to be a controversial claim. In the phrase 'Hindu monotheism', the adjective is used as a shorthand to distinguish the frame of a discourse in which the Veda is generally referenced as revelation and there is a common set of cultural and religious practices, such as making an offering to the image of a god and receiving a blessing. Hinduism is usually characterized in the popular imagination as polytheistic, with a plurality of gods, demons, and other supernatural beings represented in iconic form, to whom offerings are made for appeasement or in return for a favour. It is certainly true that there is an abundance of shrines, temples, groves, rivers, mountains, and trees, all revered as sacred and embodying a deity. Yet the major traditions of Hinduism centred on Śiva, Viṣṇu, and the Goddess are monotheisms in so far as they regard their particular focus as the supreme being, of whom other gods are manifestations or aspects. This idea came to be debated in philosophy and, as in Western philosophy, arguments developed for the existence of such a being, especially in

[1] I use standard transliteration for Sanskrit terms, except for place names and some modern personal names that are commonly Anglicized.

relation to atheist objectors. What sort of God could this be? Surely not simply another object that exists along with trees and stars but rather the source of all that exists and so, in some sense, beyond existence. Thus, arguments for God's existence were integrated with issues of causation (whether an effect pre-exists in the cause) and the very nature of inference (Lipner 1978: 62–6; Dasti 2011).

The development of Hindu monotheism, suitably qualified to distinguish it from Abrahamic religions, is inseparably linked to the emergence of a social *imaginaire* and view of the human good. The ideal of what it means for a human being to become complete has been articulated through political and social factors that favoured the dominance of a particular deity, along with the development of a philosophical discourse that reflects on the nature of the world, the person, and duty (*dharma*). Hindu monotheism is related to concerns about freedom from suffering as one of the purposes of life; to speculation about the nature of a person, especially in relation to Buddhist and Jain philosophies that rejected an ultimate transcendent source of life; and to concerns about ontology, the nature of the world itself and how the world is to be classified or categorized. All this is set within a political milieu that saw the rise of kingship and varying forms of patronage of different religions throughout the history of South Asia and a social milieu in which caste is the central social reality.

To discern a history of Hindu monotheism we must rely on textual evidence from scriptures along with philosophical reflection, as well as political and sociological evidence from inscriptions bearing witness to royal patronage, land grants to particular groups, and so on. In terms of a brief sketch, we might say that the seeds of monotheism can be found in the earliest scriptures of Hinduism, the Veda, but that it really begins to emerge during the last half of the first millennium BC and early in the first millennium AD. Out of the polytheism of the early tradition, forms of theism arise as explanation of self and world, which become the focus of worship, arguably flowering in the first millennium AD, during which time what we would recognize as modern Hinduism comes into view. From around the sixteenth century, on the eve of modernity (as in Europe), there is a shift in philosophical discourse that continues through the nineteenth century into the contemporary world with the emergence of India as a nation state.

Is Hinduism a Polytheism or a Monotheism?

It is always difficult to make broad generalizations about religions, especially one as complex and diverse as Hinduism, but a short answer to this question is that it is both a polytheism and a monotheism. With some credence, the nineteenth-century Indologist and comparative religionist Max Müller described the religions of the Vedas as henotheism, the worship of one god at a time in so far as the hymns of the text praise a particular deity as if that god were supreme and above all others (Müller 1899: 53). Certainly, in one sense the history of Hinduism can be characterized as polytheistic, but what this means must be understood in the context of cosmology. Until modernity, the Hindu cosmos, along with that of the Buddhists and Jains, was a hierarchical structure, a vast edifice within which all of life was contained – and indeed it remains so even today. The forms that we see and experience in our everyday going about the world, the plants, animals, and other people, along with invisible forms, the spirit of the tree, the guardian goddess of the village, the spirit of the spring, snake deities, the innumerable malevolent supernatural forces that seek to disrupt our life, and the benevolent deities that bless us are within this vast cosmos. At the top of this great chain of being, to use Lovejoy's apposite phrase (Lovejoy 1936), is the highest deity, variously conceptualized in different traditions. This hierarchical structure is made more complex within the history of Indic civilization through its relation to the abstract metaphysical systems of the philosophers and the political harnessing of theological ideas: a 'scale of forms' in Collingwood's phrase adopted by Inden (Inden 1990: 33–6).

This general picture of the kind I have just sketched was in place by the first millennium AD and probably much earlier. To take a brief example, the *Netra Tantra*, composed during the eighth century in Kashmir but an important text used by royalty in Nepal, introduced in 1200, lauds the deity Amṛteśvara and his consort Amṛteśvarī as supreme, forms of Śiva and the Goddess, and much of the text is about how to protect oneself and one's family, especially the royal family, from malevolent supernatural forces: to protect one's children from the evil eye through magical utterances and ritual. Much religious observance is concerned with attempting to control the interactions between humans and invisible beings, particularly the malevolent ones whom we wish to keep away. And it would be inaccurate to think that this world view is a thing of the past. Anecdotally, I can give an example of my once foolishly praising the baby of a young woman and her husband who had kindly invited my colleague and I for tea. Immediately the young woman left the house and smeared dirt on the baby's face lest my praise should attract the jealousy of an invisible demon.

This practical polytheism, the everyday religion of most Hindus, entails an understanding of what a person is that Charles Taylor has characterized as 'porous' (Taylor 2007: 35–43). The porous self is a person whose boundaries are not closed and in which external, invisible powers can come into the person – especially demonic forces – and which can also leave. This is in contrast to what Taylor calls the 'buffered self' of modernity, in which we no longer believe in such forces and the boundaries of the person are closed as an individual along with other individuals in a disenchanted world or a world of modernity characterized by the dislocation of person from wider cosmos, which Taylor calls a 'great disembedding' (Taylor 2004: 49–68). India as a modern nation state participating in a high-tech, global economy has millions of people just as 'disembedded' as everywhere else, but it also contains millions of Hindus who still live within an 'enchanted' cosmos, such as my young hosts, for whom invisible deities and demons are real; these invisible beings interact with the visible human world. Indeed, the social reality of most people in India perhaps questions a hard and fast distinction between Taylor's porous and buffered self.

But let us grant the force of the idea of the porous self for a moment. Let us call this kind of porous self, in the Hindu context, permeable. By 'permeable self' I mean that a person is embedded within a society and within a cosmos, and interacts with not only other people but with invisible powers both because of the desire for protection, that is the appeasement of those powers, and for enhancement and well-being, ultimately for the greatest enhancement of salvation from this world of suffering. The permeable self is less an individual in the sense of the modern, urban, buffered self, and more of what Marriot has called 'dividual' (Marriot 1976: 109–42). The dividual person is embedded within a social network in which duties and obligations to others are well defined, social roles are clear, and that network within an Indic or caste context is hierarchical, based on a scale of purity with some groups, the Brahmins, regarded as ritually pure while other groups, often the most economically downtrodden, are regarded as ritually impure, such as the Dalits at the bottom of the traditional scale of purity. The sociologist Louis Dumont famously distinguished between purity and power in relation to caste, with the image of the king exemplifying power and the Brahmin exemplifying purity but in which the political realm of sovereignty does not become wholly distinct from the realm of religion (Dumont 1980: 312). On this view, the king can become an analogue of deity and, indeed, is thought to embody the qualities of God. Thus we have a complex social network, a hierarchy of supernatural agency, and a politics of divine kingship in the history of Hinduism.

It seems to me that the plurality of the Indic social network is linked to the plurality of cosmic beings. Hindu polytheism is populating the cosmos with a hierarchy of supernatural entities that reflects the hierarchy of the human social order throughout history. The transactional nature of the person in that social hierarchy is akin to the transactional nature of the person in the cosmological hierarchy. As ritual procedures control interactions between people – forms of comportment towards others as well as more formal ritual procedures such as rites of passage, especially birth rites, initiation, marriage, and funeral rites – so ritual procedures control human interactions with invisible beings. Rituals protect us from evil – such as my young friend's smearing dirt on the face of her baby – honour deities, and gain liberation. Hindu polytheism is thus linked to social hierarchy as the model, the dominant theme in the social *imaginaire*, along with modes of ritual that control the interaction of the person and community with invisible cosmic powers. This is, of course, not unique to India but found throughout Asia and, indeed, throughout much of the world.

But what of monotheism, the topic of this Element? Hindu monotheism must be understood within the context of a social and cosmological *imaginaire* that is hierarchical and within a cosmos replete with invisible powers. That there is a force, the source of the universe and the beings within it, that in itself transcends that universe and social order is attested throughout the history of Hinduism. The relation of such a supreme being to the human community is mediated through the cosmical hierarchy and articulated at the human level through images, incarnations, and human embodiments. Thus, God incarnates in the world in forms such as Rāma and Kṛṣṇa and can be accessed through the media of icons in temples, and through holy men and women as themselves icons of the divine. God appears in the world in iconic and aniconic forms; simply seeing the deity is regarded as transformative of persons. Such a transcendent God has been understood through the model of sovereignty. God is like a great king ruling a kingdom or sphere (*maṇḍala*), whose kingdom is the whole universe. With God as king at the apex of the universe, below him, or sometimes her, are arranged a hierarchy of gods, anti-gods, supernatural beings such as Nāgas (the supernatural snake-persons), demons, people, animals, and plants. As we will see, this hierarchy was even conceptualized bureaucratically, as in the religion of Śiva, with different departments governed by different deities. But images of God also emerge in which he is not so much king as lover or friend.

We might generalize that Hindu monotheism is distinct from monotheism in Judaism, Christianity, and Islam in a number of important ways. It is a clear doctrine of Abrahamic religions that God is the creator of the universe from nothing. In Christianity, this God is a trinity and there was some debate about the relationship between God and his creation, God being present within it, while maintaining a transcendence from it. The interesting theological issue arises, therefore, that God is the creator of existence and so is distinct from existence: God is not just another object in the universe. We cannot understand God as an object in a way that there are other things in the universe that can be named. So, in what sense can we say that God exists?[2] Christian theology came up with a number of responses to this

[2] For a succinct discussion of this issue, see Denys Turner 2002. The atheist denial of God is a denial of understanding God as an object in a way that there are other things in the universe that can be named.

question, particularly that God does not exist in any conventional sense, but is a being only known as analogous to creatures. Hence for Thomas Aquinas, we can know that God exists but not what God is (Turner 2004: 169). God is essentially unknowable, which led the fourteenth-century Orthodox theologian Gregory Palamas to claim that God in essence is incomprehensible yet can be known in the energies that proceed from it (Manzaridis 2015: 23). Interestingly, this directly parallels the eleventh- or twelfth-century Hindu theologian Rāmānuja's claim that God in essence (*svarūpa*) is unknowable but can be known in his power (*vibhūti*) (Flood 2019: 144; Hunt-Overzee 1992: 75). In Abrahamic religions, God intervenes in history, becoming incarnate according to Christianity. In Hindu monotheism God likewise incarnates in different animal and human forms to restore righteousness. So, in very general terms, we might say that the similarities between Hindu monotheism and that of the Abrahamic religions are the following:

1 God in essence is unknowable because transcendent and so beyond human powers of understanding.
2 This transcendent God, while being beyond the universe, yet either creates or emanates it.
3 God intervenes in history through incarnations: the unique incarnation of Christ in Christianity, for example, or a variety of human and theriomorphic forms in the religion of Viṣṇu.
4 God is the controller of time: in Hindu monotheism, God governs the endless cycles of destruction and rejuvenation of the universe; in Abrahamic monotheism, God sustains the universe having created it, and destroys it at the end of time.
5 God bestows grace on devotees, saving them in the end: God has a soteriological function.
6 God is good. God is identified with the highest good in the Abrahamic religions and Hindu monotheism, although in the latter God is also ultimately the source of time, suffering, and death (as we see in the *Bhagavad-gītā* chapter 11).

Some differences between the concepts of God in Abrahamic monotheism and Hindu monotheism are the following:

1 God in the Abrahamic religions creates the world from nothing, in contrast to Hindu monotheism, where such a claim could be contested, and where God is often thought to act upon eternal, insentient matter.
2 Hindu monotheism is affirmative of images of God, whereas the Abrahamic religions are not, with some exceptions, such as icons in Orthodox Christianity.

3 The Abrahamic religions often believe that God has a purpose (*telos*) for creation, in contrast to Hindu monotheism, in which the only purpose to creation is for God to express his/her nature (and so the universe is God's 'play') or in order that bound souls can be liberated.
4 In Hindu monotheism, God rules over reincarnation through the cycles of time, the various ages of the world which repeat, an endless process although individual selves can be liberated. This is in contrast to the Abrahamic God, who will render collective judgement at the end of time.

There are other differences and similarities but at the risk of making massive over-generalizations, these seem to me to be the most significant.

Yet Hindu and Abrahamic monotheisms developed in quite distinct histories, polities, and geographies. Jan Assmann has argued that the emergence of monotheism in Egypt for a short time, and particularly in what was to become Judaism, marked a revolutionary event (Assmann 2008). But this revolutionary event was accompanied by the eruption of violence with which monotheism is associated. Assmann distinguishes pagan violence in which the king acts as God's deputy, in which there is no distinction between religion and state, with monotheistic violence that was directed against paganism (including 'the Pagan within') (Assmann 2008: 29): once there is only one God, there is intolerance of others and of pluralist views. This contrasts markedly with India, where it is not so much the rise of theism that is revolutionary but its rejection in the renunciate, and often atheist, Śramaṇa traditions such as Buddhism. As we will see, the emergence of theism in Hinduism was tied to the development of the kingdom: the king embodies the most powerful God, along with the need for magical protection of the king (and thereby the kingdom) along with narratives of royal descent (Pollock 2006: 144). This imperial monotheism was not so much a revolutionary force as a consolidation of social and political values rooted in cosmic law (*dharma*), which dealt with other traditions by absorbing them within it at a lower level.

Difference in Identity

While we can speak of Hindu monotheism, God as transcendent source, never far away in the Hindu *imaginaire*, is the idea of immanence, that God pervades the universe or is identical with it, both panentheism and pantheism. That there is one being with which all forms are ultimately identical, a single substance within which difference is conceptualized either as illusory or as aspects of that single divine substance, has been a dominant trope in Hindu discourse. Such monism or non-dualism can be strict in its denial of the reality of difference or the many; only the one is real, or its purity can be compromised in the view that the many does indeed possess some independent reality but always pervaded by the one, supreme reality. On this view, God is transcendent but nevertheless not distinct from the universe, a participative theism in which the innumerable forms of the universe are expressions of divine power that might even be conceptualized as the body of God, as in the theology of the theologian Rāmānuja.

The strict ontological distinction between God and creation that we have in the Abrahamic religions is generally absent in Hinduism, with the exception perhaps of Madhva's monotheism, in which God is wholly other and external to the universe. The universe participates in the nature of God, who, in his or her essence, may remain unknowable and beyond the universe (*viśvottirṇa*), yet whose energies either pervade matter or who is transformed as matter. In this model, the *telos* of the universe is the spontaneous manifestation of God's nature. It is this difference in identity, that God is transcendent yet also all-pervasive in and as world, that is arguably the dominant metaphysical model in the history of Hindu monotheism. The roots of this metaphysics are in the ancient texts of revelation, the Upaniṣads, a metaphysics which continues into the first millennium AD. Even strict non-dualism such as the Advaita Vedānta of the famous Śaṅkara or Abhinavagupta's Śaiva non-dualism, which holds that the only reality is consciousness, have a tendency to fall into the language of emanation. For a strict non-dualism, any distinction is ultimately a distortion of the truth, but even such strict systems tend to articulate the idea of the world as an emanation, manifestation, or appearance of the one true reality. And even dualistic metaphysical systems, such as the Śaiva Siddhānta, have an account of the universe in which the universe and selves are pervaded by God's power or energy, even though they are regarded as distinct substances. God affects the incipient substance of the universe, causing it to manifest and ultimately to retract back into itself. The difference in identity position is in some ways not far removed from Christian metaphysics, in which the universe, created by God, is pervaded by God's power; God is both transcendent and immanent although with the important qualification that in Christianity, God creates the universe from nothing, whereas in Hindu metaphysics generally God acts upon pre-existing substance and the ontological distinction is never absolute, although there is room for debate here (see Lipner 1978).

Within the spectrum of Hindu views, on the one hand we have strict monism, such as Śaṅkara's non-dualism, in which difference is an illusion due to ignorance, or Abhinavagupta's non-dualism, in which the world simply is identical with absolute consciousness, which we might even designate as ultimately atheistic positions. On the other hand, we have dualist metaphysics in which God is conceptualized as a substance distinct from world and from self and yet nevertheless acts upon world through power, as in the Viṣṇu theology of Madhva (AD 1238–1317) or the Śiva theology of Rāmakaṇṭha (*c.* AD 950–1000). Between these views we have the idea that God, while being transcendent, also emanates as universe and selves: the universe is a transformation of divine substance, as in the theology of Jīvagosvāmin (sixteenth century). This position is distinct in maintaining the relative reality of the many, of difference, while wishing to adhere to the view that God becomes cosmos and the forms of the universe are not distinct from the divine reality of which they are transformations.

In this picture, monotheism can be distinguished from monism. Monism or non-dualism, while being a very important metaphysical position, might be distinguished from monotheism in which God is conceptualized as transcendent to world, but nevertheless pervades world, immanent within it. God, outside of the universe, self-contained and wholly transcendent, is also present in the universe that he has created. The relationship between God and his or her creation is therefore either one of strict separation or one of transformation in which the universe is a transformed part of God, an emanation of God. We might therefore restrict the term 'monotheism' to dualist metaphysics and to emanationism, which conceptualizes the universe as an emanation or transformation of God, who nevertheless retains transcendence; it is this latter position that is arguably dominant in the history of Hinduism. We might offer the following diagram to represent these ideas:

	Monotheism	**Emanationism**	**Monism**
God	transcendent	transcendent and immanent	immanent
Universe	distinct and real substance	real but part of God	one substance
Self	distinct and real substance	distinct but part of, or equal to, God	identical with God

Seeing the Divine

A distinctive feature of Hinduism is the proliferation of images or icons of deities that are the focus of worship. The theological importance of the image is that through it the devotee has a glimpse of God, a fleeting sight of the divine. This seeing of the image, or *darśana*, is a key practice performed before images of deities and before holy persons. Through seeing, the devotee is thought to be transformed and enriched because seeing the image makes the mind resonate with it. Seeing can also be accompanied by hearing, and hearing the names of God or singing God's praise is the aural equivalent of the visual.

In Hindu cosmological speculation, the universe has been understood as the manifestation of divine sound and hearing the names of God as lifting the devotee to that level, to that vibrational frequency. Seeing God through the image is a foretaste of the redemption to come.

Even monotheistic Hinduism reveres many gods, making offerings of flowers (*nirmālya*) and food (*naivedya*) to their icons. Unlike Islam, Hindu monotheism has no prohibition on the production and reverence of representations of God. There might be an awareness that the icons are simply stone or wood, but it is their ritual awakening that imbues them with divine power. Hindu monotheism is never worship of an unrepresentable deity but rather to a God who can be approached through a number of traditions and paths. This is recognized in Hinduism – and has been called 'inclusivism' (Hacker 1995: 245–6) – although historically this inclusivism usually meant that other religious and philosophical views accessed a lower level of truth. Thus, Śaiva theologians might arrange different perspectives in a hierarchy that corresponded to cosmic levels of attainment or realization (Watson et al. 2013: 70–6).

The sacred image is central to Hindu monotheism in so far as God becomes visible, becomes manifested in the world, through it. Indeed, we might even say that image worship is the distinctive mode of Hindu monotheism that shows God to the community and allows the community access to that transcendent reality. As Julius Lipner observes, the sacred image is 'the enabling condition of worship' (Lipner 2017: 146). Some of these images are self-manifested (*svayam-vyakta*), not humanly made but natural phenomena regarded as gifts of the deity, while others are humanly made and follow specific rules for their formation (Lipner 2017: 147–8). Such images, as Lipner notes, are didactic, intended to bring the worshipper into relationship with the deity. There is also a sense not only that the devotee sees God in the image, but God sees the devotee. A feature of monotheism is that while the world or the concatenation of things in the world is the object of human perception, the world and human beings within it are also the object of God's perception (Williams 2012: 13–14). In some sense the subject is seen by God, who thereby sees or understands more about the subject, the devotee, than the devotee her or himself. Part of the transformative power of seeing the image is that the devotee sees themself to be part of a larger cosmos, part of a greater sense of life. The devotee sees God through the image or holy person, but God also sees the devotee, which is divine love – 'you are dear to me', says Kṛṣṇa to Arjuna in the *Bhagavad-gītā*.

While the later Hindu tradition of the Sants, influenced by Sufism, tended to reject image worship in favour of a purely internalized meditation on a transcendent God without qualities (*nirguṇa*), on the whole, image worship has been the central practice of Hinduism and the way in which a transcendent deity is accessed. Paying reverence to icons – worshipping images – is a practice that is compatible with Hindu monotheism because God is expressed and accessed in many ways. But not only is the icon conceived of as the body of God, the mantra is also the sound form of the deity. Repetition of mantras in ritual and meditation is thus a kind of contemplation on the body of the deity (Padoux 2003: 478–92). But for the Sant tradition, emerging in the northern states of India on the eve of modernity, God is conceptualized as purely transcendent, without qualities, a power beyond the universe that is yet the true home of the soul and which it is the goal of life to attain. The Sant tradition advocated a strict monotheism in which God is nameless and ineffable, beyond human understanding and yet can be attained through spiritual practice such as repetition of God's names and singing the praises of God, the verses of the Sants themselves.

These Sants, good people in the community of truth, gave voice to non-Brahmanical religious aspiration. Sants such as Kabīr (1398–1448) were sceptical that Brahmanical observance could reach God: external, ritual purity was devoid of the inner compulsion to go beyond the material universe and the attainment of saintliness was not restricted to Brahmins. Influenced by the Sufis, the Sants cut across established religious boundaries, advocating a pure monotheism through vernacular languages. Poets such as Tulsidās, Dādu, and Mīrabai recited their verse to groups of followers in community gatherings, *satsaṅga*, that challenged dominant modes of social interaction. In a sense, the Sant tradition advocated monotheism for the ordinary devotee, not the renouncer nor the Brahmin, which had a significant impact on society. Indeed, Sikhism arose out of the Sant tradition from the followers of Guru Nānak. This devotionalism to a transcendent God, whose only representative on earth was in the form of the master or guru, was anti-intellectual: God is beyond language and thought, beyond the mind, realized through devotional meditation. Today, the Radhasoami movement has inherited this tradition and challenges social caste values through denying any salvific efficacy to birth and through practices such as service and commensality regardless of social station (Juergensmeyer 1991). The utter transcendence of God in this monotheism created a space in which shared patterns of devotion cut through caste divisions. Social standing becomes irrelevant before the sheer transcendence of the divine and all become equal in the quest to go beyond the veil of suffering of this world to reach, once more, the true home of the soul. This fundamentally gnostic world view was not a revolutionary movement, but it did challenge dominant Hindu social values and still does.

We have in Hinduism a number of approaches to monotheism, and in particular the ways in which a transcendent God appears in the world to human communities. In most Hindu traditions God is embodied in the temple image but also becomes embodied in the holy person as a walking icon of God. The master or guru who initiates the disciple is an embodiment of God, either in a permanent condition of divine embodiment, as in the Radhasoami conception of the master, or in temporary embodiment for the duration of the initiation ceremony, as in Śaiva Siddhānta initiation. The guru can become the primary mediator between transcendence and worshipping community: the guru expresses the love of God and response of God to human need. Through the seeing of the master (*darśana*) or the seeing of the image, the disciple is elevated to a higher perception. The image – self-manifested, humanly made, or actually human – is the enabling condition that facilitates worship and transforms devotee.

Monotheism as Social Critique

Theologies and philosophies in India have tended to reinforce cultural mores and social forms that for hundreds of years were dominated by the intellectual voice of the Brahmins. Indic philosophical discourse is a Brahmanical discourse. Metaphysics and discussion about the nature of God did not, on the whole, question the social order and while Buddhist and Jain philosophers challenged their Hindu counterparts on rational grounds, denying the relevance of caste for salvation, for example, there was little critique of the social order as such; a political theology that envisaged a transformed social order did not develop. Of course, there are political treatises, such as Kautlilya's *Arthaśāstra* (*c.* 370–283 BC), and, as we will see, kings harnessed theology for political ends, as has happened worldwide. But, on the whole, Hindu monotheism did not develop a vision of a *transformed* social order although there is a vision of a *sustained* social order or preserving polity, articulated in books of secondary revelation, the law books or Smṛtis (Olivelle and Lubin 2017). These texts articulate a monotheism closely modelled on sovereignty with salvation envisaged in terms of freedom from suffering and the cycle of reincarnation, achieved through renunciation.

Arguably this distinction between worldly governance and social cohesion, on the one hand, in contrast to other-worldly liberation through renunciation, on the other, develops because of an understanding of time and history in which time exists over immensely long periods and, on the whole, things get worse as the ages of the world move on. This theory of the different ages of the world, the *yugas*, expresses an extended view of time in which human, historical time is but a small part. There is a constant, if non-identical, repetition of events and a constant reincarnation of the life force (*jīva*), the animating principle of bodies, into new forms over and over again. While we must be wary of essentializing cultures through too-broad generalizations – such as Indian traditions not being concerned with historical time – it nevertheless needs to be explained why, with some notable exceptions such as Kalhana's *Rājatāraṅginī*, the chronicle of the kings of Kashmir, there is a general lack of historiography in the early period: the earliest historiography in Sanskrit dating to the eleventh century (Chettiarthodi 2013). This concept of time as cyclic is a process overseen by the transcendent Lord, an image vividly portrayed in the revelation of the universal form of God in chapter 11 of the *Bhagavad-gītā*. With this general attitude to time and social change, Hindu monotheism accepted the utter timeless transcendence of God who yet orchestrates the unfolding of the cosmos through regular laws (*dharma*) and by whose grace people can be liberated from cyclic time. There is something tragic at the heart of this vision.

The Tragic

While there is an element of levity in Hindu monotheism – Śiva compared to a disguised king walking among the troops or Kṛṣṇa flirting with the cowgirls – there is also a great sense of the tragic. The human condition is one of suffering and redemption sought across vast ages. Human beings aspire to be good but so often fail; Nala marries Damayantī with the full intention of giving her security but instead gambles away all their possessions. This reflects the bigger story of the *Mahābhārata*, in which King Yudhiṣṭhira gambles away the kingdom and the ensuing strife leads to a final ironic redemption: he enters heaven only to find his enemies there before him. God is implicated in this strife and while retaining total transcendence, as we see in the *Bhagavad-gītā*, nevertheless struggles with humanity on its journey exemplified by Yudhiṣṭhira's final journey with his devoted dog (who turns out to be Righteousness).

A central image in the history of Hindu monotheism is the sacrifice. Sacrifice is an actual practice in the early Vedic period and becomes a central metaphor and literary trope. The great war of the *Mahābhārata* is a sacrifice, and renunciation is likewise a form of sacrifice. Redemption is achieved through struggle. The ascetic with an arm raised for decades so that it withers in order to achieve power over the body and the passions for the higher good, is a sacrifice. Giving up what seems to be of immediate benefit for the sake of a greater good experienced or achieved later, is an important theme along with the difficulty of achieving this and the human proclivity of succumbing to desire and passion. Sacrifice is human effort to transcend itself and to approach divinity, to become closer to God or become God-like and, in some Hindu theologies, to realize oneself as God. Transcendent God beyond the world becomes human to awaken to her, his, or its own truth. In Śaiva theology, God conceals himself but also reveals himself along with his other functions of creation, maintenance, and destruction.

These themes of tragic loss and gain, of sacrifice and redemption, are played out over the long history of Indic civilization in which monotheism is not just a theological category but a fundamental idea that animates the history of a civilization. God is beyond suffering, yet suffers with us, God is the good for which we strive, yet also the source of all things, including what we call evil. The sacrificial imaginary at the heart of the history of Indic civilization is tragic yet hopeful in its redemptive aspiration for transformation.

§

In the following pages we will examine the historical emergence of monotheism through a textual history in three moments. The first is the early post-Axial emergence of monotheism in the *Śvetāśvatara Upaniṣad* and *Bhagavad-gītā*, which articulate visions of God in what was to become the religions of Śiva and Viṣṇu respectively. The second moment is in the earlier Middle Ages, when theistic traditions had become clearly defined and were engaged in polemical debate with each other and with the non-theistic traditions of Buddhism and Jainism. Lastly, the third moment is modernity, as Hindu monotheism developed in response to Christian and Muslim monotheism and under the pressure of colonialism such that it comes to be implicated in the political, nationalist movement. Hindu monotheism today is articulated in the context of a burgeoning Indian economy, secularization, and globalization.

1 Early Hindu Monotheism

Early Vedic communities made sense of the world they lived in through ritual action, namely sacrifice, and through poetry. The two modes of understanding are intimately connected in that the poetry of the early texts was composed for and recited during ritual; the texts were performative in a very real sense. The earliest textual source of Hinduism is the *Ṛg-veda*, composed orally and passed through the generations, only being committed to writing a thousand years after its completion in around 1000 BC; the earliest manuscript dates only to 1464 AD (Jamieson and Brereton 2017: 18). The text mostly comprises hymns to the gods that were recited during Vedic sacrifice, especially the annual Soma sacrifice, the elaborate ritual to the plant and intoxicating beverage deity, Soma. Most hymns of the text are laudatory of the various gods – of the warrior Indra, somewhat akin to Thor, of the stately sky god Varuṇa, of the fire Agni, of Soma, and so on – and some hymns offer more abstract reflection, such as the famous *Nāsadīyasūkta*, which raises a philosophical question about what existed in the beginning and ends with a speculation that only the one who is the overseer of the world in highest heaven knows, or perhaps does not, although even this hymn was not simply philosophical reflection but had a ritual function (*Ṛg-veda* 10.129).

Although the hymns are liturgical in character, they are also highly literate productions as Jamieson and Brereton, the English translators of the text, observe (Jamieson and Brereton 2017: 3). Although only a single hymn, this ontological reflection is significant at such an early age, around 1400 to 1000 BC (Jamieson and Brereton 2017: 5), because it foreshadows later speculation in Indian philosophy about the nature of existence, the nature of God, and also contains the roots of scepticism (perhaps the god in highest heaven does not even exist). Generally, the hymns of the *Ṛg-veda* praise the gods, waxing lyrical about their physical and moral qualities, and about their heroic deeds, and so reflects a body of myths about them external to the corpus itself.

From these hymns we understand something of the nature of the sacrificial religion of groups of elite males, although we gain little knowledge of the wider ritual patterns of their society; regarding themselves as 'noble', theses Āryas migrated across the plains of northern India, leading a generally pastoral life with some agriculture. We know little of the ritual life of women or lower social groups at this time (Jamieson and Brereton 2017: 57–8). The function of the Vedic hymns was eminently practical. Through being praised, the gods became reciprocally indebted and needed to use their powers, so elevated in the poets' diction, for the benefit of those who praised. Jamieson and Brereton observe that this system of reciprocity was 'the dominant ideology underlying the *Ṛg-veda*, praise of the gods requires requital: they must provide recompense for what they receive from those praising them' (Jamieson and Brereton 2017: 7).

To understand the emergence of Hindu monotheism, we need to understand these ancient roots and two features in particular. Firstly, the *Ṛg-veda* was intended to be recited in ritual, or rather, the hymns themselves were completely integral to ritual action, they were not incidental; an important feature of the early religion that carries through the centuries to the development of what we would understand by the term Hinduism. The sacred texts have a practical, liturgical, or meditative function. Through the use of the text, of the sacred word, we gain access to transcendence and, in later religion, to God as the foundation of the cosmos. The later recitation of mantras in tantric religion and the singing of hymns of praise in devotional Hinduism can be seen to have their roots in these ancient hymns. Secondly, the *Ṛg-veda* bears witness to the power of the word. The poets who composed the *Ṛg-veda* had a high regard for the very nature of speech itself, the Goddess who inspires their enhanced speech is a power and her nature as power is articulated through the word. The power that is the Goddess of speech resonates in later traditions, not only in terms of right speech – the binding nature of the promise or vow – but also in terms of the power of the word to transform the person through meditative and ritual recitation, especially the power of mantras, sacred syllables, and phrases. In metaphysical speculation, the power of the word is the sound of the absolute reality, thus the idea of monotheism is linked not only to a cosmological spatial metaphor of God at the top of the manifest universe, but to a temporal metaphor of sound, inaudible to the physical ears, but heard by the inner ear within the recess of the mind in meditation: the sound of the one God that flows from and to that reality.

Systematic, sustained metaphysical reflection is absent from the early Veda, even though the seeds of later reflection are undoubtedly found here in the elevation of each deity to the highest rank for the duration of the Vedic recitation, which Max Müller called 'henotheism' (Müller 1899: 53–5). The dominating or central idea of the Veda is sacrifice, which by around the eighth century BC had become an elaborate and complex series of ritual events that followed a liturgical calendar, entailing daily offerings to the fire, sacrifices at the new and full moon, sacrifices to mark the beginning of the three seasons (hot, wet, dry), sacrifices to celebrate the harvest, and occasional sacrifices, especially the horse and Soma sacrifices.[3] Although it can be argued that the violence of sacrifice is at the heart of early religions (Assmann 2008: 32), the actual violent act of killing seems to have been less the centre of attention in Vedic sacrifice. The warrior-class patron of the sacrifice (called the *yajamāna*), accompanied by his wife, employed priests to perform the rites on his behalf, the purpose being to gain benefit for the patron, although the idea did develop that the very world itself depended upon it and is contained by it.[4] Some hymns anticipate ideas in the later Vedic corpus such as the statement in the enigmatic hymn: 'though it is one, inspired poets speak of it in many ways. They say it is Agni, Yama and Mātariśvan' (*Ṛg-veda* 1.164.46, translation by Jamieson and Brereton), the pronoun 'it' referring to 'speech', although we should be cautious not to read too much into this or project back a theological position that only developed later.

The Upaniṣads

While the Vedic hymns continue to be recited during sacrifice for millennia, other modes of literature arose reflecting on the meaning of the hymns and the meaning of the rituals they engender. Texts called Brāhmaṇa, Āranyaka, and Upaniṣad, all classified within the category of 'revelation' (*śruti*) emerged, the

[3] For a good description see Staal 1989: 65–70. See also the introduction to Olivelle 1998.

[4] See Lévi 1898: 73. *Ṛg-veda* 4.58.11: 'All the living world is firmly fixed in your domain, within the sea in your heart, within your lifespan'. There is some debate about the meaning of the sacrifice. Frits Staal, following the Mīmāṃsā tradition, regarded these rites to be meaningless but structured, syntax without semantics, rules without meaning (1989: 131–40).

core texts of the last group being composed from a period of perhaps the seventh or sixth century BC through to perhaps the second century AD. The Brāhmaṇas reflect a stage in which sacrifice had become a complex and expensive affair, while the Āranyakas and Upaniṣads offer reflection on what it all means. It is in this literature that we find what we might call philosophical speculation on the nature of an absolute reality. In the earlier texts the power behind the ritual prayers of sacrifice, called *brahman* (Cohen 2008: 46–7), comes to be regarded as more important than the gods to whom sacrifice is offered (Heesterman 1993). This abstract principle became elevated in the Upaniṣads to an absolute reality that sustains the cosmos and with which the essence of the individual self, the *ātman*, came to be equated. We see this from the earliest of this group of texts, the *Bṛhadāranyaka* and the *Chāndogya*, where the self is famously identified with the absolute reality (Olivelle 1998: 26–7). Here the earliest metaphysical speculation is not monotheistic but predominantly monistic; absolute reality is none other than the very universe itself and the beings that comprise it, conceptualized as the cosmic sound of OṂ which pervades the universe and is indeed responsible for its arising and passing away, identified with Brahman, the world, and the self (*Māṇḍūkya-upaniṣad* 1–8).

This shift from the sacrificial performance of the earlier Veda to reflection on the meaning of sacrifice has been identified with a shift from understanding the nature of persons in terms of ritual to understanding it in terms of ethics or morality. The German philosopher Karl Jaspers coined the term 'the Axial Age' to indicate this shift that, he claims, occurred across different civilizations around the first half of the first millennium BC. Scholars have more recently revisited this idea and there is a general consensus that there was such a shift at this time (Bellah and Joas 2012). What the explanation could be, is largely not addressed. This is a large topic, but for present purposes evoking the idea of the Axial age in the Indic context signifies a shift in human thinking away from simple recitation of liturgical hymns to a reflection on the meaning of those acts and the accompanying internalization of sacrifice, and thereby ritual performance, action in space and time, shifts into ethical reflection on the meaning of life and the meaning of action. Monotheism, in the sense of a transcendent creator who stands outside of the universe and may influence it, only emerges with this Axial shift or, more precisely, slightly later than that shift, reflected in the emergence of new texts that themselves are set within the development of much wider narrative traditions, such that by the first millennium AD there are fully developed monotheisms. But before we reach that point, we need to reflect on the earliest texts in which we see the emergence of monotheism, namely the Upaniṣads.

If inherent in the concept of God is the idea of a being who creates the cosmos, then we certainly have various sequences of creation narrative in the early Upaniṣads. It is questionable whether the verb 'create' (*sṛj*) has the implication of a *creatio ex nihilo* but it may well convey the idea of emanation. Lipner has shown how the question of creation in a Hindu context is inseparable from questions of causality, from a deep philosophical concern of whether or not the effect pre-exists in the cause, as a pot is a transformation of clay, some schools of philosophy arguing the affirmative, others the negative (Lipner 1978: 62–6). At this early period this question has yet to become well defined, but these early texts are operating with a notion of creation in which there is a cause of the universe and generally they present a picture in which the universe is an emanation of a transcendent source. Conceptualizing the relationship between the source of the universe and the universe itself varies across different schools later on, but at this early period, it is not sharply defined. There are several creation narratives presented that I shall describe here, leading to the important source of monotheism, the *Bhagavad-gītā* in which the 'creation' of the world is dependent upon God.

Within the Upaniṣads, then, different models of transcendence begin to emerge: the types outlined in the introduction, monism, emanationism, and monotheism. Monism is the view that there is a single reality, *brahman*, with which the universe is identical; emanationism is the view that the universe is a manifestation of an absolute reality; and monotheism is the view that a transcendent God, distinct from the universe, is its source. Generally, the earlier texts present monism and emanationism while later texts present monotheism. While we might not wish to use the term 'monotheism' for ideas of divinity in the earliest Upaniṣads, we do find here among the complexity of themes a deity who creates the world or from whom all creatures emerge. These early texts do not demonstrate a consistent, worked out theology but reflect various views current at the time, views that are linked to the particular branch of Vedic learning to which the Upaniṣad belongs.

The earliest text, the *Bṛhadāranyaka-upaniṣad*, opens in a complex narrative sequence positing various beginnings to the universe that we need to describe. The first reads: 'In the beginning there was nothing here at all. Death alone covered this completely . . .'.[5] Here death is the source of the cosmos and seems to be identified with Prajāpati, the Lord of Creatures. A little further on the text declares: 'In the beginning this world was just a single body shaped like man'.[6]

[5] *Bṛhadāranyaka-upaniṣad* 1.2.1: *naiveha kiṃcanāgra āsīt | mṛtyunaivedamāvṛtamāsīdaśanāyayā.*
[6] Ibid., 1.4.1: *ātmaivedam agra āsīt puruṣavidhaḥ.*

In this latter sequence, the cosmic man is the first being who declares, 'Here I am',[7] and then divides into two halves, male and female, and human beings were born from their union; the female half hid herself from the male half in the form of a cow and he became a bull; she became a mare and he a stallion, and so on until all creatures down to ants were created (*asṛjat*) (*Bṛhadāranyaka-upaniṣad* 1.4.4). This seems to be a fairly straightforward creation myth, but then it takes on a further layer of semantic complexity because the term *brahman* enters the text and describes the universe as his 'super-creation' (*atisṛṣṭi*), so called because he created the gods, who are superior (*śreyasa*) to him because they are immortal (*amṛta*) (*Bṛhadāranyaka-upaniṣad* 1.4.6). Here we have a creator, the giant man who split in half, yet is mortal, creating the immortal gods in a super-creation. Yet this creator does not seem to die because, the text goes on to say, he is immanent in the world, penetrating the body to the ends of the fingers, being present in the breath, in speech, and in all the senses that apprehend the world. This innermost being (*antarataram*) is the self (*ātman*) (*Bṛhadāranyaka-upaniṣad* 1.4.8). The term *ātman* is derived from the verb 'to breathe' (*an*) and so is the life force within all beings (Cohen 2008: 39), which is also particular to each (and so it might be rendered in English as 'self'). We see here that the implicitly androgynous cosmic being who comes to awareness as an 'I' at the beginning of creation, creates or forms the universe out of himself through splitting into male and female.

This narrative sequence displays a number of themes and ambiguities that are to play out in the history of Hindu thinking. We have here the idea of a creator, a source of the universe, and yet the universe is not distinct from him. This is clearly open to a pantheist reading in so far as the universe is formed from the body of this cosmic being, reflecting the earlier hymn in the *Ṛg-veda* (10.90) where the cosmic giant is sacrificed, and his body becomes the universe and society within it. And yet, in an ironic twist, this creator who creates the gods is mortal. The text does not develop this thought but leaves it hanging.

In another sequence that opens, 'in the beginning this world was only *brahman*, only one',[8] Brahman goes on to create all the classes of society as well as the law (*dharma*) (*Bṛhadāranyaka-upaniṣad* 1.4.14) and, significantly, creates sovereign power (*kṣatra*) as the property of rulers, superior to priestly power (*Bṛhadāranyaka-upaniṣad* 1.4.11). Reflecting the earlier *Ṛg-veda*, we see that society is part of the cosmic scheme whose source lies in an underlying power and that the power of kings is derived from this metaphysical power from which the universe emerges. Thus, a social hierarchy is given theological sanction, which we see unfolding in later history (see Pollock 2006: 42–3).

[7] Ibid.: *so'ham asmi.* [8] *Bṛhadāranyaka-upaniṣad* 1.4.11: *brahma vā idam agra āsīd ekam eva.*

Following the same pattern of 'in the beginning' (*agre*), yet another sequence in the text goes back to the earlier reference to the self, 'in the beginning this world was only the self, only one'.[9] Returning to the idea of the self that is implicitly identified with the sacred power of the universe, the *brahman*, is significant in bringing home the central message of this early text, the identification of the self with cosmic power. The main philosopher Yājñavalkya, whose teaching it mostly comprises, discusses with Janaka the King of Videha about the nature of this absolute. The king suggests to Yājñavalkya various ideas about its nature, all of which he rejects. *Brahman* is not speech, or life-breath, or sight, hearing, mind, or heart. Rather the true nature of *brahman* is the self (*ātman*) (*Bṛhadāranyaka-upaniṣad* 1.1–2). This self is ungraspable and can only be designated negatively by the phrase 'not, not' (*neti neti*) (*Bṛhadāranyaka-upaniṣad* 1.3.4).

So, while *brahman* is the impersonal, cosmic power identified with the self, it is also identified with the source of the cosmos and in some ways has the attributes of divinity. Indeed, as we have already seen, *brahman* is the source of the super-creation (*atiṣṛṭi*) and even in the earliest of the Upaniṣads there is recognition of *brahman* as a creator. The word *brahman* occurs in the *Ṛg-veda*, where it is the power behind or underlying sacrificial prayers (Elizarenkova 1995: 97; Cohen 2008: 47). Yājñavalkya identifies *brahman* with the absolute that itself has no source beyond it. This power is identified with sound as the essence (*rasa*) of all worlds, a metaphysical reality encapsulated in the famous mantra OṂ that occurs early in the Vedic textual corpus, identified with the term *akṣara*, which means both 'imperishable' and 'syllable', and comes to be the sound that supports the universe and is identified with the absolute reality on which it rests. Linked to this is the threefold mantra *bhūr, bhuvaḥ, svar*, 'earth, intermediate region, sky', as a statement of all that exists.[10] It is through this mantra that an early deity, the creator Prajāpati, the Lord of Creatures, creates the world.[11] Indeed, the reference to Prajāpati bears witness not only to the idea of a creator or source of the universe but also to the idea that the universe is a transformation of a single substance. Thus, in the *Chāndogya-upaniṣad*, Prajāpati 'incubates' the universe, as a bird might incubate an egg, generating forms due to the application of heat (*Chāndogya-upaniṣad* 4.17.1; see Olivelle 1998: 541 n.). Having incubated 'the worlds', the sacred scriptures of the triple Veda[12] sprang from them. He then incubated the triple Veda, from which the mantra *bhūr, bhuvaḥ, svar* emerged, and then incubated that, from which the

[9] Ibid., 1.4.17: *ātmaivedam agra āsīd eka eva*.
[10] *Taittirīya Upaniṣad* 1.5.2 adds a fourth, *mahas*, the sun. For a discussion see Cohen 2008: 58–9.
[11] *Jaiminīya Upaniṣad Brāhmaṇa* 1.23.3, cited in Cohen 2008: 59.
[12] Namely the *Ṛg*, *Sāma*, and *Yajur* Vedas.

syllable OṂ emerged as the sound that penetrates all words, as leaves of a manuscript are bored through by a pin. This is the sound of the whole world (*Chāndogya-upaniṣad* 2.23.2). Here creation is instigated by a deity but, as generally with Indic understandings of world creation, the world is not generated from nothing. Rather the creator acts upon pre-existing substance; in this passage Prajāpati incubates the universe, 'heating' the pre-existing substance from which emerges the cosmos.[13]

This idea of an essence, a reality underlying all appearances, is common in the Upaniṣads. This essence is identified with an absolute reality, the source of the universe, as well as with the self, with which it is identical, as – to use images from the *Chāndogya-upaniṣad* – sap pervades wood or salt pervades water (*Chāndogya-upaniṣad* 6.12–13). The creator god Prajāpati is one form of this underlying power of Brahman. In these texts the idea of liberation from the cycle of reincarnation begins to come into relief and linked to the idea of realizing the oneness of being and detachment from desire. Realizing, gaining knowledge or cognition of this reality, or truth through becoming detached from desire, is not simply an intellectual achievement but a liberating experience. With such realization, the self is no longer born again in this world (*Bṛhadāraṇyaka-upaniṣad* 4.4.5–7).

Some early texts refer to the person as the supreme principle. In the *Ṛg-veda* there is the aetiological story of the cosmic man from whose body the universe and even the gods arise (*Ṛg-veda* 10.90). This cosmic male person (*puruṣa*) is identified with the self by Yājñavalkya (*Bṛhadāranyaka-upaniṣad* 2.5), although the text has previously rejected this idea (*Bṛhadāranyaka-upaniṣad* 2.1–14), and in the *Katha-upaniṣad* the person is the highest principle in a list of categories that are precursors of later Sāṃkhya philosophy (*Katha-upaniṣad* 3.10–11), which or who is the highest limit and state of being (*Katha-upaniṣad* 3.11). Although the earlier texts have identified the person with the self, here the person is higher than the self. This is probably not yet a monotheism as such, for although the supreme limit of reality, the person here does not function as creator of the cosmos.

A number of themes begin to emerge in this early literature. The predominant idea is that the self is identical with an absolute power that sustains the universe and is conceptualized as the sound OṂ. There is also the creator god Prajāpati, who acts upon pre-existing substance and transforms it into the manifest universe and the creatures within it. All this bears witness to different metaphysical ideas reflected in the Upaniṣads that the redactors of the texts are incorporating.

[13] There are exceptions to this. The opening myth of the *Bṛhadāranyaka-upaniṣad* (1.2.1) has Death, who is nothing (*na kiṃcana*), creating the universe and the *Chāndogya* (3.19.1) says that the origin of the universe is in non-being (*asat*).

These speculations were probably linked to particular families within which the texts were compiled, the different branches of the Veda.[14] Thus, for example, the *Chāndogya-upaniṣad* is part of the branch of the *Sāma-veda*; it contains predominantly views about the identification of the self with the absolute power. In time this power comes to be explicitly identified with a deity who is beyond the universe and sustains it, and who is both the object of veneration and intervenes in the creation he has initiated.

In the later, verse Upaniṣads there is reflection on this single God who is the creator. The *Kena* reflects on the power that surpasses all the other gods, namely *brahman*; the *Kaṭha* tells the story of a young man called Naciketas and his encounter with death. Returning home after studying the Veda, Naciketas observes his father giving away all his possessions, including some emaciated cows, and he asks him, 'to whom will you give me?' and in irritation his father says, 'I'll give you to death' (*Kaṭha-upaniṣad* 1.4). So Naciketas goes to the house of the god of Death, who is away and does not return for three days. For his rudeness, Death offers three boons to the boy, who asks first that his father not be angry with him any more once he returns to him; secondly Naciketas asks Death to explain the fire ritual that leads to heaven; and thirdly he asks him what death is, to probe its mystery. Death does not wish to answer this last question but when pressed tells Naciketas that the secret to the mystery is that there is a primeval being (*purāṇa*) difficult to perceive, wrapped in mystery, hidden in a cave, whom one should understand as God (*deva*), and in whose contemplation one achieves freedom from both sorrow and joy (*Kaṭha-upaniṣad* 1.40). Furthermore, this is the reality of *brahman* identified with the sound OM.

This story is interesting because it shows the beginnings of a thought that beyond worldly human goods such as success and wealth, and even beyond the sacrifice that leads to heaven, there is a higher reality, a mystery hidden in the heart and perceived not through external ritual but through inner contemplation (*adhyātma-yoga*). This inner reality is indeed God and understanding this power frees the contemplator from the worldly dichotomy of joy and sorrow. This is not really a pure monotheism as the deity hidden within the cave is also the true self, and so this can be read in a monistic fashion, but nevertheless an emergent theism seems to be discernible here, a theism linked to the transcendence of the older sacrificial religion and linked to a condition of wisdom and understanding beyond heaven.

[14] The importance of the branches of learning *(śākhā)* within which the Upaniṣads were composed has been emphasized by Cohen 2008: 292: 'each of the older Upaniṣads seems to be textually, linguistically, and metaphysically more related to the other texts of its śākhā than to the Upaniṣads of other śākhās'.

This theme – almost a quest for a transcendent deity as the *Kaṭha* portrays it – is taken up in the *Īśā*, the *Śvetāśvatara*, and the *Muṇḍaka*. These texts appear to be theologically complex, on the one hand articulating a monistic vision of the self as being identical in all beings and, on the other, articulating an emergent monotheism in which the Lord is distinct. The *Īśā*, for example, describes 'the one' (*eka*) in paradoxical terms as not moving yet swifter than the mind, moving yet not moving, being far away yet near at hand, within the world yet outside the world (*Īśā-upaniṣad* 4–5). This reality 'does not seek to hide' from a man who 'sees all beings within his very self and his self within all beings' (*Īśā-upaniṣad* 6, Olivelle's translation, p. 407). Thus there is a monism here of the kind that the earlier Upaniṣads bore witness to, yet also an emergent monotheism in which there is a one both immanent (within all) and transcendent (outside all), the perception of which has soteriological value: 'in this matter what delusion, what sorrow of one who sees oneness'.[15] The term 'Lord' (*īśa*), suggesting a transcendent God, is used in the instrumental case in the opening line of the text (*īśā*) but occurs nowhere else in it. This is a semantically complex document. Paul Thieme argues that it is in fact a philosophical argument that presents a position and counterposition (Thieme 1965: 89–99), and although I share Olivelle's scepticism about this, the *Īśā* does seem to represent both the older kind of monism in which the self is identical with all selves and indeed with the world, and an emergent theism in which there is a 'one' standing beyond the world while also pervading it.

The *Śvetāśvatara-upaniṣad*

It is not until the last text of this literature, the *Śvetāśvatara-upaniṣad,* that we very clearly see the idea of a transcendent God who interacts with the universe: the emergence of a clear monotheism. Śvetāśvatara, the sage with the white mule, offers a monotheistic teaching in consonance with other texts at the time. The text has been dated by Oberlies to sometime between the birth of Christ and 200 AD on philological grounds, influenced by the *Bhagavad-gītā* and showing familiarity with other parts of the great epic, the *Mahābhārata*, such as the section about liberation (the *Mokṣaparvan*). Oberlies shows that the vocabulary of the text shares a close relation to the later language of the epics, the law books (Dharmaśāstras and sūtras), and the medical treatise the *Suśrutasaṃhitā* (Oberlies 1995: 61–102).

Opening with profound questions about how and why the universe exists, whether *brahman* is the cause or even what the cause of *brahman* is, the text goes on to explain how the Lord is perceived in inner experience through

[15] Ibid., 7cd: *tatra ko mohaḥ kaḥ śoka ekatvam anupaśyataḥ.*

meditation. In what is a significant verse, Śvetāśvatara tells us that through meditation we perceive not only God but also our true self or innermost nature along with the power of God: 'Those who follow the discipline of meditation have seen God, the self, and the power, all hidden by their own qualities. One alone is he who governs all those causes from time to the self' (*Śvetāśvatara-upaniṣad* 1.3, Olivelle's translation p. 415). Furthermore, 'the self is not God' (*anīśaś cātmā*) but, knowing God, the self is freed from all fetters (*Śvetāśvatara-upaniṣad* 1.3, Olivelle's translation, p. 415). Here the word 'fetter' is *pāśa*, a bond in the sense of a rope that ties a cow: the self, which in later tradition came to be named 'the beast' or 'the cow' (*paśu*), is both tied and freed by the Lord (*pati*), who is the cowherd. This theistic reality, distinct from the self, is found within the body through introspective meditation (*dhyānayoga*). Knowing God within, the fetters that bind the self fall away, birth and death come to an end, and in God all one's desires are fulfilled (*Śvetāśvatara-upaniṣad* 1.3). The practitioner does this through keeping the body erect and controlling the senses and the mind through the control of the breath and concentration, like a cart yoked with unruly horses (*Śvetāśvatara-upaniṣad* 1.3, Olivelle's translation, p. 415). This is a description of standard yoga procedure such as we find in the later tradition up to the present. Through concentration, the senses are withdrawn from the external world and God is realized in interiority through concentration that dispels all distractions.

There is great emphasis in the text on experience as the key to knowing God. The text describes various inner visions in the process of coming to know God and describes the positive consequences of this practice in features such as a lightness, health, a pleasant voice, and so on (*Śvetāśvatara-upaniṣad* 1.13). But, above all, through inner experience, which is knowledge of God, one is freed from bondage.

And what is this bondage? The cycle of reincarnation in which the self is driven through time, incarnating into different bodies according to its action (*karman*). This process of reincarnation, and the status of the world experienced in the condition of bondage, is referred to as 'illusory power' (*māyā*) as in the earlier Upaniṣads, but here the illusion is created by the Lord, who is like a 'magician' (*māyin*), conjuring the world (*Śvetāśvatara-upaniṣad* 4.10). Here the term 'illusory power' is identified with primal matter or nature (*prakṛti*), 'one should recognize the illusory power as primary matter' (*Śvetāśvatara-upaniṣad* 4.10), the substance out of which the universe is formed. Thus, there is a shift in the meaning of illusory power from a condition of ignorance, a perceptual distortion, to a concept of illusory power as the power of God, the very material out of which the cosmos is created. Cohen has questioned the appropriateness of Olivelle's rendering of *māyā* as 'illusory power' in an early text such as this, preferring rather calling it 'creative power' (Cohen 2008: 218). This is a good point in so far as the text does not present the idea of the world as unreal, but nevertheless it is a power that covers over the reality of God. This illusory power that is the universe is like a net that God spreads out and gathers in, creating and destroying the universe (*Śvetāśvatara-upaniṣad* 4.10), or like a spider with the threads of its web, so God covers himself with things born from primordial nature (*pradhāna*) (*Śvetāśvatara-upaniṣad* 6.10).

It would seem, then, that the text is positing a transcendent God, the Lord, along with primordial nature or matter indicated by the terms *māyā*, *prakṛti*, and *pradhāna*, which are identified with the important term 'power' (*śakti*) that comes to be central in later tantric tradition. There is also the self (*ātman*). Indeed, from the very third verse, this triad of God, power, and self is explicitly mentioned as perceived in meditation.[16] The later tradition focused on Śiva, the Śaiva Siddhānta, identifies these as distinct ontological realities. The text seems to be identifying the nouns *śakti*, *prakṛti*, and *māyā*, which are all feminine, with each other, as well s with *pradhāna*, which is neuter,[17] thereby making a strong theological point that the Lord is distinct from the material of which the universe is made. There is also a sexual connotation to this theology in that the Lord who is the unborn male (*aja*), imaged here as a male goat (*aja*), 'covers' matter as the unborn female (*ajā*) thereby producing the myriad forms of the cosmos, and there is yet another unborn male (*Śvetāśvatara-upaniṣad* 4.5) that completes the triad: unborn male God, unborn female material nature, and unborn male self.

This tripartite understanding of reality developed by Śvetāśvatara is characteristic of Hindu monotheism. There are three realities in the universe, God, matter, and selves, but the text offers an innovation here, as Oberlies shows, in that the three realities are present in two modes, the one unbound and the other bound. That is, on the one hand, from the human perspective of being bound in the cycle of reincarnation – the unliberated perspective – we have the bound soul (*jīva*), matter which is manifested (*vyakta*) as the universe, and the Lord immanent in creation, while on the other, from the unbound, liberated perspective, we have the redeemed self (*ātman*) outside of the cosmos, potential or undeveloped matter in a primal state (*avyakta*), and the transcendent Lord (Oberlies 1995: 70–1). The embodied self (*dehin*) has entered into matter, becoming covered by material qualities (*ātmaguṇa*), and is accompanied by a series of categories or evolutes of matter, namely intellect (*buddhi*) and

---

16 Ibid., 1.3: 'Those who follow the discipline of meditation have seen God, the self, and the power' (*te dhyānayogānugatā apaśan devātmaśaktim*).

17 Cohen points out, however, that because of the gender difference in the term *pradhāna* with the others, this identification is not clear. Cohen 2008: 218.

self-consciousness or the sense of ego (*ahaṃkara*) (*Śvetāśvatara-upaniṣad* 5.8). But beyond the body there is a greater part of the self that remains unbound and free from that bondage; it partakes of infinity (*Śvetāśvatara-upaniṣad* 5.9).[18]

The last element explicitly develops a view of God as standing outside the universe of which he is the source. He is without qualities, *nirguṇa* (*Śvetāśvatara-upaniṣad* 6.11), a term that is to become important as a defining feature of God in contrast to a God with qualities (*saguṇa*), who has features recognizable to humans, and is even said to have created *brahman*, the force that empowers the Vedas (*Śvetāśvatara-upaniṣad* 6.18). This God is the object of worship, who is praiseworthy and to be honoured (*Śvetāśvatara-upaniṣad* 6.5 cd). Knowing this God is redemption from the cycle of reincarnation that occurs through both the effort of asceticism and the grace of God. Indeed, the last verses claim that, 'due to the power of his asceticism and due to the grace of God',[19] Śvetāśvatara achieved knowledge of *brahman* and the very last verse mentions the word *bhakti*, 'love' or 'devotion' to God and teacher (*Śvetāśvatara-upaniṣad* 6.23). Devotion and the grace of God – clear indicators of monotheism – are new ideas introduced for the first time in the last verses of this text, and one suspects, especially as they are the last verses, that they may be later additions, although Oberlies' dating after the *Bhagavad-gītā* clearly implies that the text absorbs the *Gītā's* terminology, which includes devotion and grace. The terms 'grace' and 'devotion' are part of the conceptual universe presented by the text of a theistic reality standing outside the universe who acts upon it.

The *Śvetāśvatara* was written within one of the branches of Vedic learning, the branch of the White Yajurveda that includes the *Śatapatha-brāhmaṇa* and the *Kaṭha-upaniṣad*, and would have been conveyed within particular families who propagated an emergent monotheistic theology. Indeed, we might claim that monotheism began to emerge within specific families of textual reception, the branch of learning flowing from the Yajurveda. The philosophy or theology of the *Śvetāśvatara* brings together and systematizes different ideas within the Upaniṣads and other literature such as the *Bhagavad-gītā*. The central teaching is that God, who is the source of the universe and its sustaining power, is both transcendent and immanent. As transcendent he creates the cosmos and destroys it, and as immanent he dwells within the person, in the heart, as the central core of the self. Furthermore, through inner contemplation, focusing the mind in concentration such that the senses are controlled and withdrawn from the outer world, then knowledge of God is achieved which is a liberating experience. In

[18] See Oberlies 1995. Oberlies shows that the first chapter is concerned particularly with the tripartite Brahman, the third and fourth chapters with the description of God as Rudra-Śiva, and the fifth chapter with the two forms of the soul.

[19] *Śvetāśvatara-upaniṣad* 6.21: *tapaḥprabhāvād devaprabhāvāc ca.*

this way the text bears witness to a long tradition of inner contemplation that develops through the history of Hinduism in the yoga tradition and pervades even the traditions focused on external ritual. The text names God as Rudra, an early name for Śiva, whose lowly origins are accounted in the *Ṛg-veda*.[20] Hence the *Śvetāśvatara-upaniṣad* stands at the springhead of the tradition that was to dominate medieval India and stands at the end of a codification of theologies and the articulation of a monotheism whose broad parameters arguably become the central conception of divinity in the history of Hinduism.

This linking of liberation with an absolute reality is significant and marks the Brahmanical tradition called Vedānta from others. Jainism and Buddhism, traditions regarded as unorthodox because of their rejection of the Veda and theistic reality, certainly have a notion of liberation from the cycle of rebirth, but only in the Upaniṣads and epic literature is this freedom linked to the realization of the underlying nature of reality, of the oneness of being. The coupling of liberation with cognizing the being underlying the world is a theme in the earliest Upaniṣads. With the *Śvetāśvatara*, this liberation becomes linked to a distinct theistic reality. Here liberation is not simply down to human effort but relies on the agency of the divine being, and so the idea of grace begins to emerge, a theme that is to become important in the later history of Hinduism.

The *Bhagavad-gītā*

The *Śvetāśvatara-upaniṣad* presents a fairly consistent theology, clearly positing a monotheism which responds to and absorbs earlier material, particularly from the most important text for Hindu monotheism, the *Bhagavad-gītā*. Oberlies convincingly argues that the *Bhagavad-gītā* predates the *Śvetāśvatara*, the earliest parts being composed around 150 to 100 BC (Oberlies 1995: 67), and Ježić has identified what is probably the oldest core written in the *triṣṭubh* metre (Ježić 2009), along with layers of the text's development (Ježić 2020). Like the *Śvetāśvatara*, the *Gītā* articulates a concept of deity as distinct from the universe, who is its source, its maintaining power, and its destruction, to whom obeisance is due, and who, out of love, liberates people from the cycle of suffering. Here again liberation comes to be linked with divine agency.

The thorny theological issues associated with monotheism, such as the problem of where evil comes from if God is good, the reason why a transcendent God would create the universe, and the problem of human freedom in the light of the total dependence of our being on that reality, are articulated in these seminal texts but not systematically addressed. Both the *Śvetāśvatara* and the *Gītā* raise more theological questions than they solve, although this is perhaps

[20] Only three texts are dedicated to him: *Ṛg-veda* 1.114, 2.3, and 6.74.

true of all theistic traditions globally. In the *Bhagavad-gītā*, the warrior Arjuna gives clear reasons to his charioteer Kṛṣṇa for not wishing to participate in the imminent battle; in fighting and killing his kinsfolk, teachers, and friends, he would be going against his moral duty, his *dharma*. Laying down his bow is a clear act of human freedom, the refusal of a fate designated by his social position. Kṛṣṇa, who turns out to be an incarnation of a transcendent God, persuades Arjuna that he should participate in the battle for a number of reasons, particularly that the immortal soul cannot be killed (he would only be killing the bodies of his kinfolk), that it is his duty as a warrior to fight so as not to upset the cosmic moral order, and finally, through his cosmic revelation, Kṛṣṇa shows Arjuna that he is in fact God and that the creation, maintenance, and destruction of the universe are entirely dependent upon him. It is Kṛṣṇa who is the destroyer of worlds, the source of cosmic destruction, before whose power Arjuna is nothing. Having been given a divine eye with which to perceive this terrible and awesome vision, Arjuna asks Kṛṣṇa to return to his familiar human form. In the face of this overwhelming power, human freedom does indeed seem to be minimized and there is a sense in which the fate of the universe and all beings within it has already been determined by the fact of God's endless creation and destruction. Although R. C. Zaehner famously called the chapters following Kṛṣṇa's theophany as the greatest anti-climax in the history of literature (Zaehner 1966: 36), they nevertheless provide an additional theological insight that balances the terror of the vision of chapter 11.

This is the additional revelation of love. Arjuna, and perhaps by implication humanity, is beloved of Kṛṣṇa; he is dear to him and so Arjuna can fight with the confidence and faith not only that Kṛṣṇa will take care of the entire universal drama of the great battle, but that within this conflict and strife God loves him, a love that guarantees his final liberation, brought into the divine presence, understood differently by later theological reflection to mean becoming one with God in the non-dualist reading, or sharing in the presence of God in more theistic readings. Although the text offers a resolution to Arjuna's dilemma, that duty to the state should take precedence over duty to family (Malinar 2007: 44–5; see also Kapila and Devji 2013), it leaves other issues open, such as the degree to which Arjuna really has freedom in the face of the overwhelming power of God, and the issue of theodicy – why does God engage in this tragic manifestation of suffering even though that suffering is resolved in a state of grace?

While the *Kaṭhopaniṣad* has already presented the distinction between God, self, and unmanifest matter, with the *Bhagavad-gītā* we have clear a theistic element in the form of Kṛṣṇa at the heart of the discourse (Oberlies 1995: 72). Here is a trinity of fundamental principles, namely God, soul, and primordial matter, this latter designated by the term *prakṛti* and identified with the aspect of *brahman* that is imperishable (*akṣara-brahman*) (Modi 1932). God is the most important element of this triad as the focus of contemplation who becomes the force that acts upon the material cause of the cosmos, the womb of all being (14.3 f). The soul is a small part of God that has entered into the human body (15.7). These ideas are linked, as Oberlies observes, to different layers of the text (Oberlies 1995: 73). Matter exists in an unmanifested state that becomes manifest once God has acted upon it, and the soul becomes entangled or entrapped with manifested matter.

With the *Bhagavad-gītā* we have a clear monotheism, but one integrally linked to the earlier tradition and one that is within the sacrificial *imaginaire*. The idea of sacrifice is an important theme in the text's presentation and understanding of divinity. The universe must be understood in terms of sacrifice: creatures come from food, food from rain, rain from sacrifice, sacrifice from action enjoined by the Veda, this from the absolute power Brahman, and Brahman from the cosmic sound OṂ, thus Brahman is founded on sacrifice (*Bhagavad-gītā* 3.15; see Malinar 2003: 84–90). The whole Vedic world view is sacrificial with sacrifice at the ritual heart of the society and central to the founding myth of the immolation of the cosmic man from which society and universe emerge. Kṛṣṇa says in the text that great souls worship him with concentrated mind, knowing him to be the imperishable origin of all beings (9.13), honouring him with devotion (*bhakti*) and being always controlled, worshipping him (9.14). The two verbs used here for worship are *bhajanti* ('they worship') and *upāsate* ('they worship'), the former coming from the verbal root *bhaj*, whose semantic range includes 'to partake of' or 'to enjoy'; the latter from the verbal root *sad* with the prefix *upa*, meaning 'to sit near' or 'to approach respectfully' and so 'worship'. Worship is thus a respectful approach to God but also participation in God, as indicated by the derivation of the act of devotion (*bhakti*) and the devotee (*bhakta*) also from the same root *bhaj*. The devotee respectfully approaches and participates in, or even loves, God. These devotees who love God also participate in the cosmic sacrifice. Kṛṣṇa goes on to say:

> I am worshipped by yet others
> in the sacrifice of knowledge,
> as the one and as the many,
> manifold and omniscient. (Flood and Martin 9.15 2012)

That is, Kṛṣṇa is one yet manifests the cosmos and accepts the higher sacrifice of knowledge (*jñāna*). Indeed, Kṛṣṇa is the object of sacrifice, the one who sacrifices and the sacrifice itself. He says:

I am the rite, the sacrifice,
I am the offering, the herb,
I am the mantra and the ghee,
I am fire and oblation. (Flood and Martin 9.16 2012)

Thus, Kṛṣṇa as God is transcendent as the object of worship and the object of sacrifice yet is also immanent within the universe that itself can be understood as a great sacrifice, a great act of worshipping and honouring God. Kṛṣṇa is the father of the universe (*pitā . . . jagataḥ*), the grandfather, the mother, the object of knowledge, as well as the syllable OṂ and the sacred scriptures of the Veda (9.17). He is the goal of life, the refuge, and the friend, as well as the origin, maintenance, and destruction of the universe (9.18). He is both immortality and death, both existence and non-existence (9.19).

In these very few verses we have a succinct theology. God is the source of the universe and the beings within it, beyond the universe as the goal or focus of worship yet immanent within or, more strongly, comprising all things. The text therefore wishes to maintain the older view of Brahman as being the universe itself alongside the new view of God as transcendent, beyond the universe which he creates, maintains, and destroys. Indeed, there is an ambiguity here in that the *Bhagavad-gītā* is influenced by Sāṃkhya, a philosophy that enumerates ontological categories which maintain that matter (*prakṛti*) manifests from an unmanifest state (as we saw with the Upaniṣads). In this view, God acts upon eternal but quiescent matter to create. In contrast, Kṛṣṇa clearly states here that he is the universe and, in this view, the universe is an emanation of God.

This ambiguity plays out in later theologies; some, such as Madhva's dualist Vedānta or Śaiva Siddhānta, maintaining that God is eternally distinct from matter although its animating force, and others, such as different forms of Advaita Vedānta or the Śaiva non-dualism, maintaining that the world is a transformation of God. Both views were to generate theological debate, but the *Bhagavad-gītā* is clear about the soteriological consequence of this theology. Firstly, those who worship Kṛṣṇa go directly to him for no devotee of him is ever lost (9.25, 9.31); secondly, even if people worship other gods, in truth they worship the one God (9.23); and thirdly, God accepts any offering made with devotion (*bhakti*), be it a leaf, a flower, or water (9.26). These doctrines come to prominence in later Hinduism and contribute to the idea of inclusivism in Hinduism, that all devotional paths lead to the one God.

The idea that God is in all things, or, more strongly, that God comprises all things, has moral implications. In the end, all are potentially saved, even the wicked if they turn to face God (9.30). The text recognizes a moral order to the universe in which a process of natural justice ensures the correct balance of the deeds of each; all creatures get what they deserve and are accountable for their merits or demerits accumulated over countless lifetimes, yet through devotion and grace a person can go to God and be saved from the endless cycle. All beings are lost so long as they are not found, but once found, they are ensured peace (9.31). But at the end of the day, it is God himself who is both lost and found.

On the eve of the great battle, the theological battle lines, as it were, are drawn up over the nature of God as being wholly transcendent or immanent in and as universe, as being reached by human effort or solely through his grace, as allowing human freedom or completely controlling human destiny, and as being understood through reason or through overwhelming experience. The *Bhagavad-gītā* is a very important text for the development of Hindu monotheism. The theology of God's transcendence and immanence, of his revealing and concealing, of grace and action, of love and knowledge, are all here. Yet so are the theological paradoxes and conundrums that all theologies face: Why would God create such a universe? How can we have freedom in the face of such overwhelming power? and Why do some receive the free grace of God and others not? Later traditions developed theologies that directly or, more often, indirectly address these issues.

2 Developed Theologies

By the early centuries of the Common Era the philosophies and theologies of Hinduism were beginning to sharply formulate their positions and certainly by the eleventh century the different theologies had defined themselves against each other and against the competing atheist philosophies of Buddhism and Jainism. Hindu monotheism (if I might use the word 'Hindu' anachronistically) developed within traditions that are focused on particular gods, especially the central deities Śiva, Viṣṇu, and the Goddess (Devī). Hinduism had always been pluralist since the ancient Vedas in the sense of having a multiplicity of gods, but, as we saw in the last section, there is an emergent monotheism, a monotheism unlike that which developed in the Abrahamic religions but distinctive, in which the multiplicity of deities came to be regarded as emanations of the one God. In the constant process of deification that occurs in the history of Hinduism – of ancestors, of nature, of cultural forms such as the alphabet and language itself, and even of the bodily senses into goddesses – the multiplicity of deities came to be theologically absorbed into a number of major narratives and traditions. Local gods came to be identified with major regional and trans-regional deities, thus local, protecting goddesses that were incorporated within the mainstream tradition of the Goddess or even Kṛṣṇa of the *Bhagavad-gītā* may have originated as a local deity, perhaps a deified ancestor, in the region of

Mathura, believed to be the birthplace of Kṛṣṇa, in the process of the amalgamation of different traditions (Schmid 2010: 20–7). Local deities came to be absorbed into a larger mainstream in a process called Sanskritzation or Brahmanization. But first, in charting the history of Hindu monotheism we have to make some comment on the interrelated issues of periodization and intellectual history.

In periodizing Indian history, Western scholarship has used categories that developed from Western history, particularly the classical age, the medieval age, and modernity. Their application to the history of India has resulted in some distortion in Western representations of that history – such as seeing the pre-modern as degenerate – but the periodization is not wholly wrong in the sense that we might speak generally of a pre-Gupta age before around 600 AD that might roughly correspond to the classical category and a post-Gupta age that roughly corresponds to the medieval (see Kulke and Rothermund 1998: 103–51). But understanding history in these terms does not entail a moral evaluation that things degenerated from the classical to the dark ages, a discourse that was projected onto the history of India culminating in the idea that by the eighteenth century, Hindu discourse was weak, feminine, and lacked intellectual rigour (Inden 1990: 86, 123). On the contrary, I think we must understand Indian intellectual history as one of development in which intellectual arguments and positions become increasingly demarcated alongside a process of syncretization in which currents of thinking come together. On the issue of monotheism, intellectual debate reached a degree of sophistication and technicality equal to the development of monotheism in the Abrahamic religions. It is not that monotheism is restricted to theologians and philosophers, popular movements towards monotheism of a particular kind come to be articulated in a genre of Sanskrit text called Purāṇas, ancient narratives about the origins of royal dynasties and gods, and also in later narrative traditions in vernacular languages, but my focus here will be on intellectual history, the ways in which monotheism comes to expression in the traditions of Śiva, Viṣṇu, and the Goddess during what we can call the medieval period, which occurs principally through the medium of Sanskrit, although there are important vernacular commentarial traditions, such as those in Tamil and Malayalam.

Monotheism and Kingship

A system of social stratification or caste had become well established by the early Middle Ages[21] along with an ideal of kingship in which kings ruled over

---

[21] There is some controversy over this; some scholars argue that caste as we understand it only emerged with colonialism. See Dirks 1988 in contrast to the affirmation of caste as an ancient system by Louis Dumont 1970.

large regions where vassal states paid homage. This kind of kingship is what Burton Stein has called an embedded hierarchy, with lower kings paying tribute and honours to higher, regional rulers, as in the Vijayanagara empire (1336–1565), for example, a model distinct from the centralized, state-ruled empires such as Rome (Stein 1989; also see Peabody 2003). The functions of the king were the administration of justice (*daṇḍa*); maintaining righteousness (*dharma*), particularly understood as the maintenance of the hierarchical social order; and waging war.

To understand divinity, people have used the models of human relationship culturally available to them, and Hindu monotheism developed in conformity with the idea of Hindu kingship. Indeed, it is no coincidence that the term for god, *deva*, is also a term for king. The God who creates, maintains, and destroys the cosmos over and over again is imaged on the king ruling an embedded hierarchy of vassal states. God at the summit of creation radiates out lesser deities as local rulers might be seen to be irradiations of the great king. Thus, in the Śaiva religion God dispenses the function of creation to a vassal deity Ananta, himself the chief of seven Lords of Wisdom (Vidyeśvaras). In this cosmological model we have an embedded hierarchy not dissimilar to the model of the Hindu state that Stein has described. There were other models available too: thus, God can be understood as modelled on human relationships such as parent-child, friend-friend, or two lovers.

But this question of the relationship between monotheism and kingship is complex. On the one hand, the understanding of divinity reflects the social and political models available to a community, while on the other monotheism as theological discourse has a life of its own. There are purely theological concerns that propel the discourse about monotheism. Take the philosophical tradition of Vedānta, for example. Here a tradition based on commentaries on texts, especially the root text of Badharāyana's *Vedānta Sūtras*, begins with a non-dualist interpretation that comes to fine expression in Śaṅkara, which then moves in a monotheistic direction with later theologians (of note are Rāmānuja and Madhva). Or the philosophical arguments for the existence of God in the Nyāya school of logic respond to Buddhist arguments and those of other Hindu schools, particularly that of Vedic exegesis, the Mīmāṃsā. The degree to which we can speak of the development of Hindu monotheism independently of wider social and cultural practices and ideas is difficult to assess. Intellectual developments always occur within webs of cultural meaning and social practice, of course, and yet in turn can influence those practices, as we see throughout the history of religions. Problematics internal to particular kinds of discourse – philosophical, literary, scientific – have their own trajectories and cannot be reduced to the sociopolitical context in which they operate.

One way of approaching the problem might be to understand state formation in terms of the two axes of centralization and legislature or a system of law. Centralization refers to the state where power is located in a 'centre' where decisions about governance are made and from which power is distributed to regions. Strong centralization generates authoritarian political regimes in contrast to weak centralization where state power is attenuated. The system of law is conceptually distinct, and a legislature can develop independently of governance. As I have written elsewhere, 'a strong legal system or legislature in combination with strong centralisation generates a more authoritarian political system whereas its opposite, a weak legislature and weak or no centralisation, generates the opposite political system, namely anarchy' (Flood 2019b: 6).

The model of Indian kingship that Stein has identified implies a moderate degree of centralization although accompanied by quite strong legislation through the law books or Dharmaśāstra. Monotheism can map on to governance in so far as it implies some degree of centralization, but it can function independently of a system of law. Monotheism can therefore be associated with authoritarian rulers and various theocracies in human history illustrate this. In the history of India, there have been varying degrees of authoritarian rule, sometimes strongly authoritarian regimes have promoted a particular kind of monotheism, such as the Hoysala king Viṣṇuvardhana (r. 1110–52), famous for the temples at Halebid and Belur, who became a devotee of Viṣṇu and drove out the Jains (Stein 1989: 16). Other kings were more tolerant of diverse traditions, such as King Śaṅkaravarman of Kashmir (883–902 AD), who seems to have tolerated a variety of religions in the kingdom, even though he 'kept tight control in fiscal and religious matters' and damaged temples through plundering them and introducing draconian taxes, fines, and forced labour (Deszo 2005: 17–18). Jayanta Bhaṭṭa, who worked in the employ of Śaṅkaravarman, was concerned about new, tantric religion undermining social values and urged the king to ban certain tantric sects, which he did (Deszo 2005: 16, 20).

During the medieval period, the Hindu world (which covered South and Southeast Asia) came to be dominated by the religion of Śiva in what Alexis Sanderson has called 'the Śaiva Age' (Sanderson 2009). Large kingdoms presenting the characteristics of Stein's embedded hierarchies, rose to dominance: the Cholas and Pandeyas in the south, the Malla kings in Nepal, and the Khmer kingdom in Southeast Asia. War was a feature of these kingdoms, but also the building of large, regional temples that exhibited the king's power and patronage of particular religions. The development of monotheism occurs within this political context in which some understanding of divinity is based on kingship – God is a great king – and in which kings support different kinds of monotheism as a state religion. The Chola king Rājarāja I (*c.* 985–*c.* 1014), for example, built the great regional temple to Śiva at Tanajvur in the Tamil country, and his own kingdom, as ideal, came to reflect the universe governed by Śiva. This kind of Hindu monotheism was articulated through ritual action, especially in festivals that affirmed the king's power and the homage of the people. Indeed, one Śivadharma text tells us that on the occasion of the copying of a scripture, a great festival was held with a procession to the temple and that the populace would adhere to the religion of the monarch (Sanderson 2019: 34).

During the Gupta period (third century AD–*c.* 600), during which the royal dynasty of that name dominated northern India, Hinduism as we might recognize it today begins to emerge, with devotion (*bhakti*) to various deities, each understood as a kind of monotheism, expressed in narrative texts called Purāṇas that also contain mythological histories and information about ritual practices (Bisschop 2006). These texts were not technically regarded as examples of revelation (*śruti*) but rather of inspired human tradition, remembered texts (*smṛti*) that might nevertheless be regarded as a secondary revelation. These texts continued to be composed to about the eleventh century, when we have the important and highly influential *Bhāgavata-purāṇa*, a text – like the *Bhagavad-gītā* – concerned with Kṛṣṇa, but this time with Kṛṣṇa as a playful incarnation of a transcendent God on intimate terms with his devotees as a lover with his beloved (Hardy 1983). This Kṛṣṇa *bhakti* religion developed within the context of the flowering not of the religion of Viṣṇu, but of Śiva, which gained royal patronage among the kings of India during the medieval period. I shall take up the development of late Vaiṣṇava monotheism in the next section, but we first need to understand the full flowering of monotheism in the religion of Śiva.

Śaiva Monotheism

From around the eighth to the thirteenth century, roughly the post–Gupta period, the religious history of South and Southeast Asia might be characterized as the Śaiva age, as Sanderson has established. In Kashmir there was a particularly significant flowering of Śaivism, and another in the south, where the Chola kings in particular were responsible for its propagation. This religion permeated all levels of society from kings to Brahmins, to commoners. At one level there were the Brahmins, whose worship of Śiva was based on the Purānas and who followed rules of purity laid down in Vedic scriptures and Vedic law books, as well as lay devotees of a non-initiatory Śaivism found in the Śivadharma literature, but a kind of Śaivism also developed based on a new revelation in texts called Tantras, a tradition that called itself 'the path of mantras', the Mantramārga (for an overview, see Sanderson 2019). A mantra is a phrase or sentence that embodies a god, the sonic equivalent of the visual icon (Padoux 2003), which the Tantras articulate. These texts generally took the form of a dialogue between Śiva and the Goddess, teaching the various forms of Śiva, how to worship him, and how to gain liberation and power. The initiatory religion of Siva, known as the Śaiva Siddhanta, the 'system or tradition of Śiva', which follows the teachings of Śiva (Śivaśāsana), was the dominant tradition taught in the Tantras. Alongside this Veda-congruent religion, there were traditions that rejected its social conformity, arguing that liberation from the cycle of reincarnation along with power and pleasure in other realms of existence could be achieved through transgressing orthodox boundaries and going beyond the restrictions imposed by Brahmanical purity rules. These transgressive religions, the more extreme tantric religions, often revered the highest theistic reality as the Goddess and proffered a monotheism in a path of the Goddess religion, the Kulamārga.

Thus we have four kinds of monotheism developing: first, the popular, highly orthodox, Veda-congruent tradition of the Purāṇas, which extol particular gods as supreme, along with popular Śaivism expressed in the Śivadharma literature; second, the Veda-congruent Śaiva Siddhānta that reveres a new revelation from Śiva encoded in the Tantras; third, a Veda-rejecting path within the Mantramārga that is generally non-theistic; and fourth, the Goddess-orientated Kulamārga in which the Goddess, ruling alone, replaces the male god-king. This tradition of focus on the Goddess is an important historical trajectory and it is important to remember that theism is not restricted to male deities (see Bose 2018: 1–4).

Alongside popular cultural articulations of monotheism and the initiatory religion of the Śaiva Siddhānta that spread throughout India with royal patronage, there developed a sophisticated philosophical discourse that included debate about monotheism. Within this lively discussion over generations through learned commentaries on both revealed texts and independent philosophical works, some philosophers from within the orthodox or Vedic horizon supported theism while others, both within the Vedic horizon and outside of it, rejected the idea. Kashmir was a particularly rich area for the development of discussion and during the medieval period philosophical discourse reached a high level of sophistication.

The Śaiva theologians of Kashmir developed theologies principally through commentary on revealed scripture. While there was some debate about the validity of new revelation, whether this was even possible, most accepted this new development and the new religion of Śiva came to be accepted within courtly circles (Sanderson 2009: 254–73). Śaiva theologians began to reflect on the meaning of these scriptures and two major intellectual trajectories developed, the dualist Śaiva Siddhānta that argued for the transcendence of God, distinct from matter and souls, and the non-dualists who argued for their ultimate identity. These arguments were formed against a soteriological backdrop of a Śaiva Siddhānta belief that liberation is attained through ritual effort following initiation and the grace of Śiva, and the non-Siddhānta belief that liberation lay in recognition of one's identity with Śiva or the Goddess. These non-Saiddhāntika religions were focused on the Goddess as well as Śiva and might therefore be considered as Śākta-Śaiva, in contrast to the Śaiva Siddhānta, which was focused on Śiva without a consort in the form of Sadāśiva.

While Hindu monotheism closely follows the model of kingship, this is not to say that there were not purely intellectual and even emotional reasons for its development. The intellectual, Brahmanical elites who composed texts and systematically thought about philosophical and theological issues, generated arguments in support of different kinds of monotheism, refuting the claims of rival schools. Within the Śaiva horizon, dualist Śaiva Siddhānta theologians argued for the transcendence of God against non-dualist Śaivas who propagated monism, yet whose arguments embraced monotheism as a lower level of understanding. There were also earlier arguments for the existence of God within a purely philosophical framework in the school of logic, the Nyāya, that came to be absorbed and reworked by the Śaiva Siddhānta theologians. The monotheist philosophers thus find themselves having to argue against the orthodox, atheist tradition of Mīmāṃsā, against the Śaiva monists, and against the Buddhists. In some ways, all of these three traditions might be characterized as atheist philosophies in either their rejection of the idea of a transcendent creator or their relegation of theism to a lower, simpler level of understanding. I will here sketch these developments firstly by presenting an account of Nyāya arguments for the existence of God and how these came to inform Śaiva arguments for theism and secondly present an account of the monists' response, all this set within the Buddhist rejection of both theism and an ontology of self.

The Philosophy of Monotheism

During the 9th – 10th centuries there was rigorous debate about the existence of God (Īśvara) and the nature of God in Indian philosophy. The school of logic, the Nyāya, developed arguments for the existence of God that are close to Christian and Islamic parallels. These Nyāya philosophers thought that the existence of God could be established through argument alone, without reference to scripture (Dasti 2011: 1). The Nyāya philosopher Udayana wrote a rational justification for God's existence – a form of cosmological argument – as did Jayanta Bhaṭṭa. Indeed, Jayanta's humorous play, *Much Ado About Religion*, lampoons the various religious factions in Kashmir, reflecting the rigour of philosophical debate at the time (Bhatta 2005). Ratié has shown how the proof of God's existence first seems to have been used in lost works of the Nyāya philosophers, whose arguments become elaborated by later Nyāya authors such as Jayanta Bhaṭṭa and

Udayana (Ratié 2016). Indeed, the most important theistic arguments were presented by the Nyāya against both Mīmāṃsaka theorists, who accepted the revelation of the Veda, yet maintained atheism, and the Buddhists, who rejected the Veda alongside the idea of God. Praśasta seems to have been the person responsible for introducing the notion of a creator God who, like a supreme administrator, ensures the correct retribution for actions (Bronkhorst 1996). Furthermore, these rational arguments for God's existence are not simply regarded as dry, academic debates; rather intellectual understanding was thought to have soteriological impact (Moise 2017).

The Nyāya argument is generally that the universe is of the nature of an effect. If this is so, then all effects have a cause, and we can infer that this cause is a theistic reality. We can infer God as cause from the natural effect that is the universe. Udayana presents several arguments along these lines (see Bhattacharya 1961; Chemparathy 1972). First of all, the universe is an effect requiring a cause. It comprises a specific arrangement (*sanniveśaviśeṣa*) that must have been created by an intelligent agent because no material cause can account for that specific arrangement. Because of the complexity and harmony of the universe, we can infer that this intelligent agent must be an omniscient and omnipotent being. This argument was taken up the Śaiva philosopher Utpaladeva and has been well described by Ratié, who cites and translates Utpaladeva's text, as well as the texts of his opponents to whom he responds (Ratié 2016). Although at the end of the day, Utpaladeva was a non-dualist, he nevertheless wrote a book arguing for the existence of God and defending this doctrine against its atheist detractors, even though he regarded it as a lower level of truth than his non-dualism.

The Mīmāṃsā school of philosophy was a tradition of exegesis, looking into the nature of revelation and the nature of language, although the revelation it conceives of has no author and is eternal. The first proponent of this view, who wrote the school's foundational text, the *Mīmāṃsā-sūtra*, was Kumarila. In response to the argument of the theists, that the universe has the nature of an effect from which we can infer an intelligent causal agent, he questions the force of the theists' analogical reasoning. The theists argue that the specific arrangement that is the pot requires us to infer the intelligent agency of the potter, and similarly the specific arrangement that is the universe requires us to infer the intelligent agency of God. But, thinks Kumarila, the pot is either the product of the potter or the product of God. If the former, then the fact that the arrangement that is the pot is in itself insufficient, because the pot perishes, does not prove an imperishable God. Furthermore, if God is to be compared to the potter, then God would be perishable as the potter is. If the latter, the creator of the pot is God, then this likewise does not establish the case because God has never been seen to create a pot. This objection is further developed by the Buddhist philosopher Dharmakīrti, who argues that one can only infer a particular agent from a specific arrangement when on earlier occasions it has been seen to be causally dependent upon that agent (Jackson 1986; Hayes 1988). If this were not the case, one could infer that an anthill was produced by a potter simply because it is made of clay. There is only a superficial verbal similarity between the cases of the anthill and the pot, which is insufficient to establish God as the cause of the universe (Ratié 2016).

Utpaladeva defends creation by God against both the Hindu atheist Kumarila and the Buddhist atheist Dharmakīrti. Against the former, he claims that inference does not establish a specific agency but rather simply demonstrates the invariable concomitance (*vyāpti*) between an entity with a specific arrangement of qualities and a cause that must be an intelligent being. This cause is then particularized, as when we see smoke above a group of khadira trees, from which we infer that there is a fire there. But we then need to particularize this as a special type of fire, a khadira fire. In a similar way, we can infer the cause of the universe, which has the qualities of harmony and complexity, to be a necessarily omnipotent and omniscient creator. The omniscience and omnipotence of the universe's cause can be inferred from the complexity of the effect that is the universe. Utpaladeva argues against Dharmakīrti's point, reminding us that we can infer the existence of a particular cause, a potter, from a particular arrangement, a pot, when we can infer their invariable concomitance. 'Invariable concomitance' is a technical term in Indian philosophy that means that two things, such as fire and smoke, invariably go together; where there is smoke there is probably fire, and we can infer a causal connection between them. Thus, we infer particular instances of fire as the cause of smoke even if we cannot directly perceive the cause. There has to be, he says following Jayanta, some degree of generality – as in the claim that fire, in a general sense, is the cause of a particular emanation of smoke. Likewise, with God: God can be inferred as a cause in general because all inferences involve generality and all particular effects share a partial similarity in being specific configurations (see Ratié 2016).

These arguments affected Śaiva Siddhānta thinkers, although their reflections are also based on the Śaiva revelation that itself is aware of these debates. Śaiva Siddhānta theologians propagated monotheism within a wider context of practice and general revelation of Śiva. Revealed texts such as the *Parākhya-tantra* (pre-tenth century AD), offer some intellectual argumentation for the existence of God. This is an important dualist Tantra that presents an argument that the universe has the nature of an effect of which God is the cause. Proceeding by a process of critiquing earlier positions, the text is set as a dialogue between

Prakāśa, the sun, and Pratoda, a name for the sage Vasiṣṭa (Goodall 2004: xl), who asks Prakāśa various questions and is led to an understanding of the doctrine of God through a process of reasoning. In its treatment of God, the text first advances the Mīmāṃsaka view that the universe has always been and that the cause of the universe is action or karma: that 'the form of the earth is thus; it was never not thus'.[22] This is rejected on the grounds that karma could not be sentient and that the cause of the universe would need to be sentient because of the need to particularize entities into what they are. I take this to mean that the results of past action alone cannot account for such differentiation in natural phenomena because if it is unconscious force, then there would be a sameness to its effects. The retributive force of past action cannot be the cause of the universe, although it could be used by a causal agent to make the particular arrangement that is the universe. If the force of action is indeed a force, then it would need to be directed by causal agency.

Pratoda inquires further. If God is infinite and outside of time then there could be no temporal sequence. So does the effect that is the universe come about at a particular time or all at once (Parākhya 2.20)? Prakāśa replies that all effects have causes and that in the case of God, the effect that is the universe is both gradual and simultaneous because the power of God being present, all effects inevitably arise. The Lord has innate power to create all effects, as there is power in a magnet, 'even though it is devoid of the instruments of the senses' (*Parākhya* 2.25–26b).

What is at issue is the nature of causation. The world being material must have a material cause, but the Lord is immaterial, and so there needs to be a material cause along with an immaterial one. In fact, there is a triad here, the Lord is the instigating cause, an auxiliary cause being the instrument through which the universe is achieved, and the material cause is the subtle matter out of which the universe is formed (*Parākhya* 2.29 abc). In his notes Goodall cites a most interesting text in support of this idea of threefold causation. God (*īśvara*) in his sovereignty (*aiśvarya*) contains the powers of knowledge (*jñāna-śakti*) and action (*kriya-śakti*), which are the instigating cause of the universe, achieved as a transformation of subtle (*sukṣma*) matter that in turn is acted upon by the Lord. The power of action is invisible and has to be inferred, as is the power of the faculty of the eye (*Parākhya* 2.36), and through this power the Lord instigates effects that comprise the universe, namely bodies, faculties of sense, and worlds. The levels of the universe are worlds inhabited by different kinds of embodied beings. (*Parākhya* 2.39–40).

22 *Parākhya* 2.12ab: *kṣirer evaṃ vidhaṃ rūpaṃ na kadācidanīdṛśam*. Goodall 2004: 169 n. 114 presents an interesting account of the phrase's history.

Against the pantheistic view that God is the material out of which the universe is made, the Śaiva Siddhānta maintains a strict theism in which the Lord is transcendent but acts upon matter in its quiescent state to produce the universe, or, more specifically, to make the universe unfold in a sequence of hierarchical levels from a pure realm, through varying degrees of subtlety, to the impure realm within which exists our universe of solidified matter. If God were the material cause out of which the universe is formed, he would be subject to transformation and therefore would be insentient. Conversely, if a sentient God were the material cause, creation would be sentient, which it is not (apart from the sentient beings within it). The commentary cited by Goodall goes on to say that even were one to accept that the universe is an apparent transformation of consciousness (as the non-dualist Śaivas maintain) then it would not be real, but the universe is real, as established by the accepted means of knowledge (Goodall 2004: 176). Thus, the Lord cannot be the material cause of the universe.

In the Śaiva Siddhānta scheme of things, God acts upon pre-existent matter when it is in a quiescent, potential state (called 'the drop' or *bindu*), which then unfolds as a graded hierarchy to a subtle material substrate of the universe (called *māyā*) that itself unfolds to a more solidified material substrate (called *prakṛti*) which forms the basis of the material world (*bhū*). The universe is a transformation of subtle matter. Within what is called the pure universe are eight deities, the Lords of Wisdom or Vidyeśvaras, the chief of whom is Ananta, who agitate primal matter (*Parākhya* 2.127). It is Ananta who acts to create the lower, impure universe below the level of its material substrate or *māyā*. Ananta is the instigating cause and *māyā* is the material cause of the lower universe (Goodall 2004: 176 n. 128).

The Śaiva Siddhānta presents a complex monotheism in which Śiva is God, omniscient and omnipotent, who acts upon matter in potential to create a hierarchical universe within which is arranged a hierarchy of powers. Śiva dispenses his power to lower deities whose function is to enact the lower creation and who have the function of helping souls to be saved from their suffering. It is a universe conceptualized in terms of a bureaucracy in which different officers have different functions, modelled on the notion of the medieval state and state apparatus. Indeed, the Lords of Wisdom are called 'office-bearers' (*adhikāriṇah*) (*Parākhya* 2.124) and they perform the five functions or actions (*pañcakṛtya*) of creation, compassion, destruction, maintenance, and obscuration (*Parākhya* 2.123–4). It is through them that the transcendent Lord has affects in the lower universe.

The theologically interesting idea that God creates, maintains, and destroys the universe, as well as concealing and revealing himself, is relegated to gods who are distinct yet dependent upon the Lord's power. We might see the five functions as a theological way of addressing questions of theodicy and the purpose of creation. Questions arise as to the purpose of such an elaborate cosmological structure. Why would God create the universe in this way? The answer perhaps can be found in the five acts of God, who conceals himself in creation in order to enact the revealing of himself in liberation. Souls, whose nature is, like Śiva, omniscient and omnipresent, are restricted and confined in the lower universe by cosmological forces, such as the 'coverings' over the soul of limited agency, time, destiny, as well as the force of their own past actions or karma, which has no beginning. Thus, one response to the question of why God creates the universe is that he does so in order that souls can achieve liberation from their bondage. God is the cause that joins the soul to the body, which itself is connected to limiting cosmological principles; the soul is impotent (*akartṛtva*) and the Lord, through his power of will (*icchā śakti*), attaches the soul to a body in order that it may consume the accumulated fruits of its past actions (*Parākhya* 4.66–8). Souls, which are innumerable, are entrapped and their progress towards God is blocked by bonds of accumulated action, which are known as impurity (*Parākhya* 1.50). The soul is the subject of experience who endures through time. Indeed, because of this the soul must be all-pervading because it experiences the fruits of its actions in a different body and in a different place. If the soul were simply a form, it could not experience the results of its action in a future birth, because form perishes; if, on the other hand, it were without form it could only be led to where the result of an experience is, because it is all-pervading (*Parākhya* 1.38). The soul must be all-pervading in order to experience the results of actions within any particular stream of time (although as they are omnipresent they in fact must exist in all streams of time). To Pratoda's question that perhaps there is just one knower, situated in bodies as the moon is reflected in water, Prakāśa replies that souls are divided because of their diverse experiences which arise from their past actions. But these experiences are ultimately delusion for the true nature of the soul is transcendent knowledge (*Parākhya* 1.42–3). Once the soul wakes up to the truth that its bondage in the world is, in the end, an illusion, it realizes its all-knowing character. And how does this occur? Through the grace of God and the regime of Śaiva ritual practice.

This economy of salvation is a complete system involving a relationship between three eternally distinct realities, God, the universe, and the individual soul. The universe is a hierarchically ordered structure that evolves from and dissolves back into its eternal material substrate. While the phenomenal universe that we experience has a beginning and an end, due to the power of God, the material out of which it develops does not; that has existed with God for all eternity. Souls are in their true nature all-pervading and all-knowing but bound within the universe due to the force of their action. At the dissolution of the phenomenal universe, they go into a quiescent state until the universe develops once more due to the Lord's power of action.

In the parallel tradition focused on Viṣṇu, called the Pāñcarātra, the place to which the souls return is called the 'Unchanging Person' (*kūṭastha puruṣa*) known as 'the beehive of the souls' (Schrader 1916: 60); once creation begins again, the souls emerge from their quiescence to become entangled in it once more, as bees fly out from their hive. There can, however, be liberation for particular souls who realize their all-knowingness and that their bondage is illusory in comparison to their condition of true knowledge. This can occur through the grace of God articulated in initiation or by following a regime of daily ritual practice until liberated through God's grace at the end of life. It is then that they transcend limitations, revealing their powers of knowledge and action (*Parākhya* 1.4, 2.70–1) and understand their true nature as being equal to Śiva although not identical with him; this is no pantheism but a hierarchical ordering of cosmos and the beings within it.

The Non-Dualist Argument and Monotheism

Thus, we have a philosophical trajectory that develops rational arguments for God's existence and even cuts across specific traditions with Śaiva philosophers using Nyāya arguments in support of their monotheism. The central Nyāya argument – the argument from design – was adopted and developed by the Śaivas such that Śaivism came to have an extremely strong intellectual presence.

We know so little about the institutions within which these philosophers worked; there must have been royal patronage, an infrastructure of copying texts, an industry of producing manuscript materials such as ink and palm leaves or birch bark for writing on (De Simini 2016), libraries (and library administration), and students to listen to lectures. But we do know that the philosophers read each other's work. Thus, Utpaladeva was familiar with the Nyāya philosophers, particularly Jayanta, and, of course, with the counterarguments of the Buddhists, particularly Dharmakīrti (Jackson 1986).

Within Śaivism the non-dualists of the Recognition school, the Pratyabhijñā, absorbed monotheism as a lower level of revelation. Indeed, the main bone of contention between the two traditions seems to have been metaphysics and the nature of God. The non-dualist Śaivas accepted the cultic practices of the Śaiva

Siddhānta, the shared, probably pan-Indic, ritual base of occasional rituals such as initiation along with daily ritual for salvation, but reinterpreted these and added their own supererogatory practices, particularly those coming from Goddess-orientated traditions that were often transgressive of Vedic purity rules, in the belief that transgression of social mores leads to a higher liberation, namely identity with the Goddess, who is also an impersonal power of pure consciousness. These forms of religion were ultimately pantheistic rather than theistic, and theologically read scriptural revelation through the lens of their non-dualism.

While it might be fair to call the non-dualist Śaivas of the Pratyabhijñā 'atheists' in the sense that for them the highest revelation is that the self and world are in essence identical with God, it would not do justice to the nature of their claim in the sense that there is a lower level of revelation in which the language of theism operates and is valid at its own level. Ultimately, this is transcended by the non-dualist claim which is not simply an argument but a realization that there is an identity or sameness of flavour between self and Lord. Thus, while we can speak of grace in terms of the descent of the Lord's power (*śaktipāta*) upon the devotee, this is just a figure of speech for ultimately this is a recognition (*pratyabhijñā*) of one's identity with the ultimate source of that power. Recognition of the self's identity with God became the marked feature of this philosophy, propagated in arguments by the school in response to both the dualistic Saiddhāntikas and the Buddhists.

The intellectual trajectory of which Utpaladeva is a part began in Kashmir with Somānanda (c.875–925), whose *Vision of Śiva* (*Śivadṛṣti*) is an exposition of non-dualism that Śiva is the only reality, as gold is the reality in different jewels (Torella 2016: xv). There cannot be a difference between consciousness and objects because objects could not be known unless they shared the same nature or principle. All things in the universe share the same nature, which is self or the nature of Śiva (*śivatā*). Torella observes that Somānanda follows the teachings of a non-dual Śaiva religion known as the Trika that distinguishes a triad of powers – will, knowledge, and action – which are never really separated and which manifest as universe, like waves (Torella 2016: xcii). This is a non-dualism close to emanationism in the sense that the universe of apparent distinction between subject and object is a consequence of the waves of power flowing from Śiva. But Somānanda is careful to distinguish this position from the Vedānta, which regards the world to be an illusory appearance of Brahman due to ignorance, and from the Consciousness-only school (Vijñānavāda) of Buddhism that, while accepting the unreality of objects, denies the reality of the subject of knowledge (Torella 2016: xviii). This is the distinctive flavour, as it were, of this kind of non-dualism. The world is not an illusion or a shadow but is the full and complete totality of the consciousness that is Śiva.

Somānanda's indirect disciple, Utpaladeva, was one of the most original propagators of this metaphysics along with his intellectual descendent, the very famous Abhinavagupta (*c.* 975–1050 AD). It is curious that Utpaladeva should write a book defending monotheism, arguing that the universe is an effect (*kāryatvāt*) that therefore needs a cause (Ratié 2016: 259), but his verses on the recognition of God (the *Īśvarapratyabhiñā-kārikās*) and his auto-commentary on his text constitute his distinct contribution to this philosophy. In this book he developed a non-dualist understanding of God, that God is none other than the totality of the universe and the beings within it, along with all the invisible beings and worlds that exist on more subtle levels in a hierarchical sequence. Thus, while accepting the cosmology of dualist Śaivism, he presents a non-dualist interpretation of it. Indeed, as Torella observes, the main thrust of his argument is against the Buddhists rather than the monotheist Siddhāntins. After presenting an exposition of the Buddhist position as a critique of the realist Nyāya, he then goes on to demonstrate the inadequacy of the Buddhist view, which does not appreciate the relationality of the universe driven by the dynamic force of Śiva.

While Utpaladeva and his non-dualist colleagues assumed the Śaiva Siddhānta cosmology, the metaphysics they produced is quite distinct. Rather than the static identification of the self (*ātman*) with the absolute (*brahman*) found in the early Upaniṣads, as we saw above in the first section, the Śaiva non-dualist metaphysics is organized around the metaphor of light. The universe that we experience is not distinct from God, its source, in one way of speaking. The universe is an appearance of light. The term *ābhāsa*, meaning 'appearance', is from a verbal root meaning 'to shine', and the absolute reality in this system is conceptualized as light (*prakāśa*) and self-reflection (*vimarśa*) (Torella 2016: xxvii–xxviii; Ratié 2011: 116, 382–7; Dyczkowski 1990). This light is consciousness and none other than a cosmic sense of 'I' (*ahantā*), reflected in the indexical use of 'I' in everyday discourse and also in the objects of experience that are its manifestations.

The Pratyabhijñā introduces a dynamic understanding of God as self-reflexive consciousness with which the universe and the beings who inhabit it are ultimately identical. This is not a monotheism in the sense of the Śaiva Siddhānta, for which the three distinct realities of Lord, self, and universe are so distinct as to veer towards a gnostic attitude to the world as something that the soul needs to escape in order to find its peace and liberation with God. While still operating within the Indic paradigm of reincarnation, the Śaiva or Śākta-Śaiva non-dualist imbues everyday experience with value in the sense that the fullness of experience through the senses is in reality the fullness of God's experience of himself, or indeed herself as the essential cosmic unity of consciousness is also referred to in terms of the Goddess. For Abhinavagupta and his student Kṣemarāja, the Goddess is the esoteric, pulsing heart of the system and of the universe itself.

South Indian Devotionalism

The basic Śaiva system that developed in Kashmir took root in the rest of India, too, taking a particularly robust form in the south, where it became infused with devotionalism (*bhakti*) and the additional scriptural language of Tamil. While the Tamil sources recapitulate the Sanskrit revelation, they place emphasis on devotion that itself comes from Tamil devotional poetry. Using Śaiva metaphysics as an intellectual backdrop, the emphasis here is on the emotional experience of being overwhelmed by God and the immediacy of experiencing God directly, as can be articulated through poetry. This emotionalism had wide appeal and the ancient styles of Tamil poetry came to be used to articulate a devotional monotheism in which the devotee is subordinated and overwhelmed by the otherness of a transcendent God. Indeed, the tradition of Tamil poetry existed before the advent of Sanskritization in the south, collected into a number of anthologies called Caṅkam literature, and so it is possible to derive a history of Hinduism from a focus on Tamil tradition. The Tamil deities Mudvalan and Tirumål became identified with Śiva and Viṣṇu, Korravai the goddess of war with Durgā, and the important deity Murugkan with Śiva's son Skanda, the god of war.

The Tamil tradition expressed in the early literature prior to the third century impacted upon the Śaiva Siddhānta. The poetry of the sixty-three Tamil Śaiva saints known as the Nāyanārs came to be regarded as scripture along with the Tantras. The ritual tradition came to be overlaid with a layer of devotionalism in which the direct relationship between the devotee and the Lord is emphasized, alien to the spirit of the earlier tradition, in collections of poetry: the *Tirumurai*, the *Tévāram*, and Mānikkavācakar's *Tiruvācakam* ('Sacred Verses') (sixth–eighth centuries). Here the devotee is 'mad' (*piccu*, *unmatta*) with the love of God. These poets sing songs of praise to Śiva embodied in the temples of the south which became a network of pilgrimage sites during the period of the Chola kings (*c.* 870–1280).

Such devotionalism also found articulation in other Śaiva traditions. The Liṅgayat community in Karnataka, which is ultimately derived from a Śaiva ascetic group called the Pāśupatas who belonged to the 'Higher Path' or Atimārga division of Śaivism (Sanderson 2019), developed devotional poetry in Kannada. One famous female devotee, Mahādevyakka, wrote in an intimate tone about Śiva as her beloved, rendered as 'My Lord White as Jasmin' in Ramanujan's masterly rewriting:

> I love the Beautiful One
> with no bond nor fear
> no clan no land
> no landmarks
> for his beauty.
> So the Lord White as Jasmin is my husband.
> Take these husbands who die,
> decay, and feed them
> to your kitchen fires! (Ramanujan 1973: 134)

Mahādevyakka is depicted as a naked ascetic, covered only with her hair, going against social mores that become subordinated to the love of God. The highest purpose of life is not worldly success or the affirmation of the everyday values that we see in the system of the purposes of life (*puruṣārtha*), where duty, prosperity, and pleasure are legitimate human goods to be pursued, but a rejection of those values in favour of a transcendent goal. Śiva is here not a domesticated deity but retains his feral characteristics on the edges of the social order to emphasize his utter transcendence of the world.

Between the sixth and ninth century, Tamil tradition also focused on Viṣṇu. Devotion to Viṣṇu was articulated by poet saints called the Alvars in a collection of Tamil poetry called the *Tiruvāymoli* assembled by Nammālvār (*c.* 880–930 AD), which contains 1,000 verses of songs to Viṣṇu under his Tamil name Māyôn ('the Dark One'). He is both king and lover, not unlike Kṛṣna, reflecting old Tamil poetic genres of poetry of love (*akam*) and war (*puram*). Indeed, this text became so important in the Tamil tradition that it is called the 'Tamil Veda' (Carman and Narayan 1989). The Alvars' songs were sung in temples and placed great stress on God embodied in the temple icon, worshipped with music and dancing, and accompanied by the overwhelming emotion of longing (*viraha bhakti*). God in these texts is not so much king as intimate companion or even lover. This tradition continued through to the twelfth century, especially in the Śrī Vaiṣṇava devotional tradition. Here the renowned theologian Vedāntadeśika or Veṅkatanātha (1268–1369) expresses devotional sentiment to Viṣṇu, the Lord of Gods, conceptualized as a young child, with Viṣṇu's consort as his mother:

> O Mother who dwells in the lotus
> I make of you this small
> humble request
> grant me this favor:

that this Lord of Gods, your beloved, might listen to my words
as you would
the prodigious
prattling
of a little child. (Hopkins 2007: 48)

This tradition of devotionalism was accompanied by a rigorous theological discourse about the nature of God. Within the Vaiṣṇava tradition, two theologians in particular are significant in the history of Hindu monotheism, Rāmānuja and Mādhva.

Vaiṣṇava Vedānta

The Vedānta tradition of philosophy, flowing from the Upaniṣads, offered commentary on ancient scriptures and independent works of philosophy. One of the most famous philosophers was Śaṅkara (scholarly consensus puts him between AD 650 and 800), who promoted a monism and the identity of self with absolute reality (Brahman), a position that was rejected by later theologians of the school, in particular Rāmānuja (traditionally dated between AD 1017 and 1137), who developed a 'qualified' non-dualism, and Madhva (AD 1238–1317), who was a dualist in maintaining a radical, unbridgeable distinction between person and God. For Rāmānuja, God is transcendent in his essence (*svarūpa*) but present in the universe in his accessibility to the human community and present within the self as the inner controller (*antaryāmin*). At liberation, the soul becomes free from the cycle of rebirth and participates in the energy of God, a philosophy that became known as a qualified non-dualism (*viśiṣṭādvaita*) (Dasgupta 1975: III.165–201).

For Rāmānuja, God is transcendent and yet also the life force that animates all sentient and insentient beings. Indeed, Rāmānuja's theological project sought to maintain the utter transcendence of God while yet promoting God's immanence in the world and his participation in the created order. To preserve God's transcendence, he denied that the world is a transformation of God in essence, arguing rather that the relationship between God and world is analogous to that between the self and the body. As the self is to the body, so the Lord is to sentient and insentient existents (*śarīrīśarīrabhāva*). The universe is the body of God and we are part of that body (Rāmānuja 1953: 1.1; Lipner 1984; Hunt-Overzee 1992: 63–83). In this way Rāmānuja seeks to maintain the total transcendence of God alongside the immanence of God in the universe and the concomitant affirmation of the world (Bartley 2002: 79; Ram-Prasad 2013: 77–115): this is a panentheism in which the world has positive value because imbued with the presence of God.

Another way to preserve the utter transcendence of God is to maintain God's wholly otherness, that God is quite distinct from the created order. This is the theological move that Madhva makes in maintaining a total ontological distinction between God, world, and self. He presents a strict dualism (*dvaita*) in which the soul remains eternally distinct from other souls, from the material universe, and from God (Dasgupta 1975: IV.150–60). The universe is not illusory and contains five relationships or types of difference, between each self and God, between God and insentient existents, between individual selves, between selves and insentient existents, and between distinct insentient existents (Sarma 2003: 50–74). This theology posits difference as a defining feature of world and God and the relationship between them is of eternal distinction, even though God has the power to act upon the world and save souls. Indeed, this a doctrine of pure grace: the soul is saved entirely by grace and no effort on its own part can redeem it, a doctrine not dissimilar to that of Calvin (Sarma 2003: 90–3).

Both Rāmānuja and Madhva were within the Vedānta school of philosophy and responded against the non-dualism (*advaita*) of the earlier tradition in commentaries on scriptural texts, particularly Bādarāyaṇa's *Brahma-sūtra*, a foundational text of the Vedānta tradition. These well-articulated Vaiṣṇava theologies came to be important influences on modern Hindu monotheism and also influenced popular devotion. With devotionalism expressed through poetry in vernacular languages, monotheism became a social force. This does not mean that other gods would not have been revered, but that in the Tamil or Kannada conceptual universe God, understood as Śiva or Viṣṇu, is the transcendent source and goal of life; this source is conceptualized as the king but also the beloved, the regal but also the intimate, the transformation of life but also the salvation from life.

The extent to which monotheism has been a social and political force in the history of Hinduism is an important question for understanding the history of political and social formation. On the one hand, as with Śaivism, monotheism tended to support the status quo and rule by the political elites, as we see in the adoption of Śaivism as the official religion by so many kings, from Kashmir to the Khmer kingdoms, during the medieval period. Yet, on the other hand, in terms of personal devotion it has touched the lives of ordinary people, not only initiates. For Basava (twelfth century) in Karnataka, monotheism implied social and political equality, such that the Liṅgayat community rejected Brahmanical social stratification, although the riot against King Bijjala II was perhaps more a populist eruption than a political programme with a sustained agenda. Clearly the ideology of devotion supports the idea that all are equal before a transcendent God who proffers grace to humankind. But, apart from among the Liṅgayats, monotheism did not become associated with a desire for a new social order; indeed, it tended to reinforce the social order through legitimizing the power of kings and the understanding of the universe in terms of sovereignty. Both Śaiva and Vaiṣṇava theologians understood God through this model of kingship. Hindu monotheism underwent changes with the two large incursions of Indian history: the Muslim dynasties, especially the Mughal, and the British empire. Hindu monotheism developed through these political changes and through the impact of modernity to the present time, a development to which we now need to turn.

3 Hindu Monotheism in Modernity

By the mid-thirteenth century the Śaiva age was at an end. This is not to say that Śaivism faded away, it remains to this day a vibrant religious force, but tantric Śaiva states came to an end, with the exception of Nepal, which retained its tantric-kingly connection until the demise of the monarchy in 2016. Following the Delhi Sultanate (1206–1526), the Muslim Mughals became the dominant political force, ruling most of northern India until their downfall and the rise of the British, perhaps marked particularly by Clive's victory over the Nawab of Bengal and his French allies at the Battle of Plassey in 1757. But the Hindu kingdoms were not completely eliminated. The Vijayangara kingdom that had arisen in response to the Delhi Sultanate lasted until the early seventeenth century (Stein 1989: 109–39) and the kingdom of Jaipur flourished with Jai Singh II paying tribute to Aurangzeb. The tantric Hindu kingdoms were replaced by the Muslim Delhi Sultanate and, following that, the Mughal empire. In terms of Hindu intellectual development, Vaiṣṇava theology came to the fore with important theologians, especially towards the end of the medieval period: as we have seen, Rāmānuja and Madhva composed important theological works within the Vedānta tradition supporting different kinds of Vaiṣṇava monotheism. And Islamic monotheism had some influence on Hinduism through the Sufis, who impacted on the Sant tradition in the north, exemplified by poets such as Kabīr and later Nānak, devotional songwriters who operated outside courtly circles. This devotional movement, from which Sikhism arose, focused on a transcendent deity. Indeed, vernacular religious poetry in Hindi became important in expressing devotion not only at a popular level but in the Mughal court (Busch 2011), and Sants such as Nāmdev became important in creating 'publics of memory' which still have an impact today (Novetzke 2011). Under British colonialism, Christianity had some influence on Hindu monotheism in the nineteenth century, stimulating what became known as the Hindu Renaissance; thinkers such as Rammohan Roy and Vivekananda absorbed Christian values in the service of a reassertion of Hinduism. Some Hindus became Christian and developed a Hindu-influenced Christian monotheism, such as the Tamil-speaking A. J. Appasamy (Dunn 2016). But let us begin with Hindu monotheism as it developed in the shadow of the Mughal empire.

The Love of God

Hindu monotheism came to articulation in different genres of literature, from philosophical treatises to works of popular devotion, during the medieval period and we have examined some examples in the previous section. Of note, a kind of emotional devotionalism (*bhakti*) develops, characterized by longing for God, as we see in the eleventh century *Bhāgavata Purāṇa*, which became, and remains, immensely popular (Bryant 2017). In this text Kṛṣṇa is not the kingly figure of the *Bhagavad-gītā* but a lowly young cowherd brought up by his surrogate mother Yaśodhā. This Kṛṣṇa-Gopāla, who originated as a tribal god, and his brother Balarāma were pastoral deities who came to be assimilated into the mainstream Vaiṣṇava tradition (Schmid 2010: 20–3). In this tradition Kṛṣṇa, a prince threatened by his wicked uncle Kaṃsa, was whisked away from danger to be raised in the idyllic rural setting of Vrindaban. Here, Kṛṣṇa is an erotic young man, playing flirtatious tricks on the cowgirls, stealing their clothes whilst they bathe in the river and climbing a tree so that they must appear naked before him to implore him to return their garments. The tenth element of the *Bhāgavata Purāṇa* describes Kṛṣṇa dancing with all the cowgirls in a circle dance, each one thinking that he dances with her alone (Bryant 2003).

This theologically interesting story illustrates a fundamental feature of devotion to God through a form, namely that for each devotee the relationship to God is unique and particular. This is a kind of personalism in which the devotee is entirely focused on God in the form of Kṛṣṇa but, furthermore, Kṛṣṇa also appears to be entirely focused on the devotee. The devotee loves God as the cowgirl loves Kṛṣṇa and that love is reciprocated. As seeing an image of deity gives access to its reality, so the cowgirl beholding Kṛṣṇa and entranced by him has direct access to God and moreover is in turn seen by God: Kṛṣṇa too is entranced by the cowgirls and both he and they are absorbed in mutual love, passion, and devotion. Each gives to the other what each has to give, namely themselves and their love. These tales illustrate not only how the devotee sees God but how the devotee comes to self-awareness through being seen by God: devotees have the look of someone who is looked at (Williams 2012: 13, using a metaphor by T. S. Eliot).

It was to this kind of passionate, devotional religion that a young Brahmin named Caitanya converted. Born into a Brahmin family that gave him a standard, Sanskrit education, Caitanya (1486–1533) rejected traditional religious forms and the idea of liberation through knowledge, claiming rather that uncompromising love of God leads to salvation, through his grace. After performing memorial rites for his deceased father in 1508, he had a transformative personal experience with a south Indian renouncer who initiated him into the worship of Kṛṣṇa. Caitanya developed a form of worship that stressed love and devotion by repeating the names of Kṛṣṇa, and through ecstatic dancing and singing Caitanya experienced enhanced states of mind, 'possessed' by God. In 1510 he and his followers moved to Puri in Orissa, where there is a large regional temple to Viṣṇu in the form of Jagannātha, the Lord of the Universe. There, Caitanya and his disciples would follow the great processional carriage each year, singing the Lord's praise (Stewart 2010; Wong 2015). Fundamentally anti-intellectual and even potentially transgressive of caste boundaries, this devotionalism attracted a broad base of followers. Caitanya died at a fairly young age leaving behind only a few verses of poetry but his legacy was the movement that he founded, known as Bengal Vaiṣṇavism, part of which became the modern Hare Kṛṣṇa movement. Although he did not formally begin a school of theology through writing a commentary on the *Brahma Sūtras*, he is nevertheless regarded as the founder of this tradition. He taught that Kṛṣṇa is God and not simply an incarnation and his followers came to believe that Caitanya himself incarnated both Kṛṣṇa and Rādhā (his favourite cowgirl in later tradition) in one body.

Although Caitanya emphasized openness to the grace of God through emotional devotion rather than intellection, within his lifetime the movement developed strong theological reflection, articulating theology in traditional ways through commentary on sacred scripture and some independent works. Within Caitanya devotionalism grew a theology headed by a family called Gosvāmins. The brothers Rūpa and Jīva relocated from Puri to Vrindaban, the place where the incarnation of God in Kṛṣṇa was believed to have taken place (Gupta 2007: 121–3). Of particular importance was the Gosvāmins' identification of aesthetic experience with religious experience, something that Abhinavagupta had done previously within the Śaiva tradition.

One of this new religion's themes was reflection on the love of God. How do we understand the love of God by devotees and God's love of persons? We have seen how models of divinity are dependent to some extent on human relationships, in particular the idea of the king in the earlier period. With Caitanya's movement, theological reflections came to focus on other ways to model the human-divine connection, in particular using the image of two lovers as depicted in the *Bhāgavata Purāṇa*. In the history of Sanskrit poetic literature, there had been a tradition of expressing human love, especially the passion of two lovers in a situation of forbidden love, the love of the adulterous affair (Seigel 1978: 137–77; Leinhard 1984). Here there was a distinction between love in union, which takes place within marriage and is characterized by desire (*kāma*), and love in separation, which occurs in adultery and is characterized by pure love (*prema*) and longing (*viraha*). Kṛṣṇa's favourite cowgirl Rādhā is an older, married woman who falls in love with him, drawn by the irresistible sound of his flute (Seigel 1978: 116–20). The soul's love and longing for God is akin to Rādhā's love and longing for Kṛṣṇa, a love that transcends worldly desire and obligation: she leaves behind a shadow of herself in her husband's bed when she departs the house to be with Kṛṣṇa in the forest. Our bodies act in the world to perform our duty, but our souls fly away to God in another place.

This is a simple image and immediately identifiable, the lover's longing for her beloved is just like the longing of the soul for God. This is a very personal and intimate monotheism, a monotheism in which devotee and God are both vulnerable before each other and where separation is an ontological reality, experienced as longing (*viraha*), along with the emotional suffering it brings in the knowledge that the lovers must part come the dawn. We are a long way here from the theological reflection of Rāmānuja or Nyāya arguments for God's existence. God is directly perceived as the object of longing and desire, an object of love. Of course, inevitably, the theologians took this primal human experience of love and turned it into sophisticated theology. Rādhā becomes Kṛṣṇa's 'refreshing power' (*hlādinī śakti*) through which the cosmos is manifested, distinct from him as the 'possessor of power' (*śaktimat*); Rādhā as his power and his lover is united with him while remaining distinct, as the soul will be united with the Lord in salvation while remaining distinct. This is a monotheism in which God is transcendent and yet in intimate relationship with devotees, a theology that came to be known as 'non-difference in difference that is inconceivable' (*acintyabhedābheda*) (Gupta 2008: 51–5; Frazier 2009: 168–71).

Reimagining the relationship between God and person, which is what the Gosvāmins were doing, is also to reimagine the end goal of redemption. At liberation, the devotee participates in the worlds of God in different forms according to its proclivities and orientation – as lover, friend, parent, or servant – and in this participation might be said to partly merge with God, while the true nature of God remains transcendent. This love is also service (*seva*) for in loving God the devotee serves God. Indeed, redemption is the freedom to serve God absolutely, perhaps as a friend, but equally perhaps as a blade of grass bending with the breeze in God's highest heaven: at death and final liberation, the devotee takes a form most appropriate to their love and for their service. The impersonal absolute of the Advaitins is not denied in this theology, but relegated to a lower realization, the truth of God is that he is wholly transcendent as Lord (*bhagavān*). To worship God through offering devotion (*bhakti*) is to participate in his being while remaining distinct and this is experienced through overwhelming and unconditional love.

Political Theology

But this theology caused some consternation. In the Kachvāha kingdom of Jaipur, Mahārāj Jai Singh II (1688–1743) maintained his kingdom's independence from Mughal rule, although he always preferred diplomacy over conflict of arms. Jai Singh saw himself as a good Hindu king and wanted a state religion that articulated his and the kingdom's Hindu identity, for which he turned to the religion of Kṛṣṇa. But he was troubled by the theology of longing and the image of love in separation as the religious ideal, because, arguably, it was fundamentally immoral and went against *dharma*. Goddess Rādhā was surely not a role model for women in his state (see Pauwels 2009). He therefore employed theologians to look into the matter. Hence Bengal Vaiṣṇava theology was given courtly sanction during his reign. Jai Singh wished to turn Kṛṣṇan theology into a kind of political theology that would support his vision of the Hindu state and act as a bulwark against Islamic power and Islamic monotheism (Patel 2018): Hindu monotheism was just as good if not better. We must be wary of transposing Western terms onto the eighteenth-century Jaipur court, but we might call Jai Singh's concern with monotheism a kind of concern about political theology because it regarded the intellectual justification of doctrine to have public and political impact.

Jai Singh II was committed to religious reform and the coherence of social and political orders by reinforcing orthodox Brahmanical values of duty with regard to stage of life and social group (*varṇāśrama-dharma*), the four estates of Brahmins, warriors or nobles, commoners, and serfs, but with reference to devotion to Kṛṣṇa. Jai Singh was concerned to maintain a strong state with conformity to public morality and social order in which the king was at the top of the hierarchy alongside the Brahmins, and citizens were arranged below this in varying degrees of status. In establishing a strong state and unequal power relations within society, Jai Singh drew on Hindu literature such as the epics *Mahābhārata* and *Rāmāyana*, and even himself authored a treatise on Rām, the ideal king. He also saw himself as akin to Yudhiṣṭhira, the great king in the *Mahābhārata*. Within this conception of sovereignty, *dharma* was a central ideal. Jai Singh wished to integrate religious obligation with obligation to the state, to which end he held court debates and employed theologians to write learned treatises (Patel 2018). For example, as Patel has shown, Kṛṣṇdeva moulded together devotion (*bhakti*) with adherence to ritual action (*karma*) and adherence to social obligation (*dharma*). Drawing on his teacher Viśvanātha, he agreed that *bhakti* is the ultimate goal of practice, but nevertheless ritual action was important at a lower level; this entailed the integration of religious observance with the maintenance of social order along with the support for the king and state (Patel 2018: 103, 109). This was a monotheism in which the king's justice reflected the cosmic justice of God. Jai Singh was keenly interested in the limits of ritual action and social obligation. At what point would or could the devotee abandon ritual action and what consequence could this have for the devotee's loyalty to the state? Furthermore, what are the moral implications of devotion to a God who seems to disrupt conventional morality in his incarnation as Kṛṣṇa?

These questions were never completely resolved since the devotee who loves God might well neglect their obligations as citizen to the state without committing a sin from a purely theological perspective. Yet Jai Singh wished to promote a monotheism in which devotion to king and state paralleled love for God and in which love of God did not go against Brahmanical cultural values and adherence to the social order of caste and stages of life. The image of illicit love in the theological tradition as an image of the love of the devotee for God was therefore understandably disfavoured by the king (Wong 2015: 318; Horstmann 2009: 98–120; Burton 2000: 111–15; Okita 2014).

Jai Singh's polity is a good example of the way in which theology was not simply restricted to the monasteries or systems of religious education but rather had a place in the public sphere. Theology was part of public discourse and its findings had a bearing upon political matters. It is not that theology had been in the private sphere and governance in the public (there was no Lockean distinction between private religion and public governance), but theological discourse had a life of its own independent of political regimes. With Jai Singh we have the harnessing of theology in the interests of the state in a move that echoes the Mughal state apparatus where monotheism under emperors such as Aurangzeb sometimes became a political tool for the occlusion of Hinduism.

Indeed, a striking feature in the history of Hindu monotheism is that little overt political theology was written. There is no equivalent to Augustine's *City of God* (De civitate dei) in the Hindu tradition. Arguably this is because of Hindu views of time as cyclical and the understanding of salvation as transcendent, but also because scriptural revelation is itself thought to be ahistorical in the sense that the Veda has no beginning and, according to strict Vedic tradition, is without author. The redemption spoken of by the Gosvāmins, and the love of

God they extol, transcends state formation and does not attempt to accommodate it, although the state might attempt to cultivate a favourable monotheism as we see with Jai Singh. But the social relevance and importance of monotheism was to develop much more in the nineteenth century, especially in response to colonialism.

Monotheism as Response to Modernity

From the mid-eighteenth century, British rule began to be established in India and was consolidated by the nineteenth. The British colonial presence exposed indigenous religions to Western modernity (Wong 2015: 319). Because of the colonial power differential, in one dominant line of thinking Hinduism was in some ways 'constructed' as a 'religion' (Fitzgerald 2000: 134–46; Inden 1990: 85–130) and Hindu monotheism during this period, especially in Bengal, inevitably responded to the power dynamic, both in terms of being influenced by Christian thought and in terms of reacting against colonialism to establish a distinctly Hindu understanding of God. This is a complex historical period during which monotheism comes to articulation in new ways. While it is not possible to be comprehensive, I would like to identify two currents of Hindu theological reflection in the modern period, one distinctively modernist in its attempt to mould Hinduism into a monotheism modelled on Christianity and Islam, the other distinctively traditional in its resistance to modern and colonial ways of thinking. We can call these simply 'modernist' and 'traditional' theological orientations.

We can identify the modernist theological orientation as beginning with Rammohun Roy (1772–1833). Roy, founder of the Brahmo Samaj, was a monotheist, deeply influenced by Islam and Christianity, who attempted to push Hinduism in an overtly monotheistic direction (Crawford 1987; Killingley 1993). To develop Hindu monotheism, he translated the Upaniṣads into Bengali and English, encouraged debate, and pressed for social reform. He modelled his form of Hinduism on Unitarianism, with which he had come into contact and which resonated with his thinking and rethinking of the Hindu tradition, to reject image worship, reject some aspects of Hindu society such as caste, child marriage, and the ritual burning of widows, and to create Hinduism as an ethical spirituality equal, or even superior, to Christianity and Islam. In this philosophy, God is known through reason rather than through revelation, which also led to the discovery of universal ethical codes, although for Roy there is a limit to reason's knowledge of God because he is 'eternal unsearchable and immutable Being, who is the author and preserver of the universe' (Collett 1962: 471). Roy published an essay in Persian, the *Tuḥfat al-Muwaḥḥidīn* (*A Present to the Believers in One God*), offering a rational argument for monotheism, that God is known through reason and such knowledge has the power to transform society and nation. Indeed, this is an important point: for Roy, monotheism is not simply about private belief but is a truth that should have affect in the public sphere, in our comportment towards each other, and should be reflected in social moral standards, even translated into law, and Roy's work was instrumental in eventual legislation against the practice of widow burning known as *suttee*. Monotheism provides the ethical imperative behind his drive for social reform.

While Roy might be described as a Hindu deist, thinking that the existence of God can be known through rational argument, he was also immersed in the scriptures of Hinduism and knew the scriptures of Islam and Christianity. As Hatcher has observed, this emphasis on ancient scripture, especially in his Bengali writings, provided sanction for Roy's polemic against image worship (Hatcher 2008: 24). It is the scriptures at the source of the Vedānta tradition, the Upaniṣads, that give us knowledge of the supreme being who is the source of the universe and its animating principle, providing the basis for good living and benevolence towards each other (Hatcher 2008: 25). Adherence to such a monotheism entails rejection of later scriptures, especially the Purāṇas and Tantras that advocate iconic worship of multiple deities – a dangerous polytheism – even if the proliferation of worshipful forms is thought to be the manifestation of a single, supreme being. Along with the rejection of polytheism, Roy refused to accept any suggestion that God incarnates in the world, rejecting both the Hindu idea of the 'descent forms' or *avatāras* of God, and the Christian idea of the incarnation in Christ (and so rejecting the Christian idea of the Trinity). Roy provided a distinctively new kind of Hindu monotheism, one influenced by Christian deism, but which he sought to root in the soil of ancient Hinduism, a monotheism not relegated to the private realm but consequential for politics and the shape of the wider community.

This idea was institutionally articulated through the society Roy founded in 1828 to promote his vision of Hindu monotheism, the Brahmo Samāj (Hatcher 2008: 22); it is a social vision that continues to this day but whose influence has been attenuated by wider cultural forces of image worship and pilgrimage within Hinduism, which Roy had designated under the sign of superstition. Another important group splintered off from the Brahmo Samāj in 1839, the Tattvabodhinī Sabhā comprising a number of key intellectuals, including Debendranath Tagore, the father of the famous poet Rabindranath. Meeting weekly to promote non-idolatrous worship and discuss theological and social matters, they saw themselves as being part of the Vedānta tradition; they regarded themselves as fulfilling his legacy on monotheism and social reform. Rather than the renunciation of the world of earlier kinds of Vedānta, as we have with Śaṅkara, for example, the

Tattvabodhinī Sabhā promoted the legitimacy of worldly interests: God is active in the world through the affirmation of social values and high ethical standards. As Hatcher has shown, the society endorsed material prosperity as well as promoting spiritual fulfilment in what he has called 'bourgeois Vedanta' (Hatcher 2008: 25). This movement fit well with the emergent prosperity of certain segments of Bengali society: British-educated Bengalis in Calcutta, who came to be known as the Bhadralok or 'cultured people'. This group were nationalist in orientation yet accepted and welcomed modernization, understood as technological advancement and scientific knowledge brought by the British, a rich soil that nurtured intellectuals such as the immensely important Swami Vivekānanda (1863–1902), a key figure in the promotion of Hinduism as an ethical spirituality and in bringing the vision of Vedānta to the West. His theology cannot be described as monotheism but as a vaguer idea that the divine exists within all beings and the world, a force that cuts across social divides, through which we can become united (Paranjape 2015): seeing God in all beings as their essence produces social harmony and tolerance.

But rather than describe this further development of the paradigm of modernist monotheism that became so important in the nineteenth century and the development of Indian nationalism, I wish to turn to another current of theological thinking, the traditional theological orientation. With the modernist orientation that embraced the new and looked to the future, an Indian future that was beginning to be imagined beyond British rule, a more traditional way of thinking also developed in Bengal that reacted to these modernist tendencies. A stricter monotheism came to be articulated by Gauḍīya Vaiṣṇavas, partly in reaction against the more pantheistic view of the Neo- Vedānta and against modernising tendencies of the Badralok. This new theology, which was also a vision of India, came to articulation in the work of the Gauḍīya Vaiṣṇava theologian Kedarnath Datta Bhaktivinod (1838–1914).

Bhaktivinod inherited the Vaiṣṇava theological tradition that promoted a monotheism of a God with qualities (*saguṇa*) in contrast to the Advaita Brahman as impersonal and without qualities (*nirguṇa*), while recognizing that this is a lower level of understanding and attainment. The kind of inclusivism that Bhaktivinod engaged in saw all theological positions as legitimate within a limited sphere, but considered them to fall short of the truth of monotheism as understood within the Gauḍīya tradition revealed by Caitanya. On this account, as Wong shows, Bhaktivinod took the essence of various theologies, becoming a 'grasper of their sap' (*sāragrahī*), and shaped theology in response to his particular circumstances. Thus, he says in his first book on Gauḍīya theology, the *Datta Kausthuba* written in Sanskrit, that a theologian should take the essence from all texts as a bee takes the essence from flowers

(Wong 2018: 14–19). Indeed, Bhaktivinod was universal in his inclusivity, embracing a range of traditions or guru lineages, the *sampradāyas*, that include ritualists, gnostics, and devotees, as well as traditions from other countries beyond the borders of India.

Within this theological vision, therefore, Christianity and, most significantly, Islam, have a place but as lower articulations of the monotheism revealed within his own tradition (Wong 2015). Bhaktivinod associated different religions with different levels of revelation and consequent realization. Thus, he describes five types of religious eligibility arranged hierarchically that map onto five levels of desire or love of God, from slight attraction to complete possession by longing for God, an overwhelming emotion characteristic of the Gauḍīya religion. These five types are governed by the three qualities (*guṇa*) that control the universe, namely goodness or light (*sattva*), passion (*rajas*), and darkness (*tamas*). In various combinations they produce the five levels, in ascending order, of darkness, passion-cum-darkness, passion, passion-cum-goodness, and goodness (Wong 2018: 17).

Bhaktivinod represents a kind of Hindu monotheism that is traditional in so far as it requires initiation into the religion by a master, followed by a regime of daily practice (*sādhana*) throughout one's life, yet is also modern in its universalising tendencies and emphasis on religious experience. In many ways Bhaktivinod's inclusivism is not dissimilar to that of Vivekananda in that both incorporate other religions as lower levels of understanding, a feature of Hindu monotheism found in the medieval Tantras. Yet this Gauḍīya monotheism is also exclusive in denying ultimate salvific efficacy outside of its initiatory structure. To know and love God in the highest sense is to be initiated into the tradition and to practice the intimate love of God taught within the tradition. This kind of religion developed with later gurus – Bhaktivinod's sons became gurus in their own right, especially Bhaktisiddhanta Saraswati (Sardella 2013) – and continued into the twentieth century, finding particularly important articulation with Prabhupada, who can be described as a monotheist theologian (Goswami 2012: 138–45), the founder of the International Society of Kṛṣṇa Consciousness (ISKCON). This form of Hinduism was exported to the West and reimported to India drawing on the monotheism of the Sanskrit tradition of theologians such as the Gosvāmins and also vernacular Bengali treatises.

The Hindu Renaissance exemplified by Rammohun Roy articulated a rational monotheism that rejected 'idol worship' and advocated an ethical spirituality as the foundation for the nation, while, on the other hand, a Hindu theistic trajectory that emphasized a Hindu, Vaiṣṇava monotheism, desiring to return to a pure monotheism where God is worshipped through the image, developed in Bengal with the work of Bhaktivinod and other Vaiṣṇavas. Swaminarayan in

Gujarat similarly advocated a monotheism in which the transcendent Lord is embodied in the guru of the tradition. These kinds of monotheism took on board a distinctively Hindu culture. The modernist and traditional theological trajectories share a desire for inclusivity in the sense of absorbing other religions and philosophies at a lower level. This is an old feature within Hindu traditions that we find in early Śaivism, for example (Watson et al. 2013), and is a feature that the scholar Paul Hacker characterized as inclusivism (*Inklusivismus*) (Hacker 1995: 244–6), a style of thinking that embraces other modes, often antithetical views, into a coherence, relegating other views to a lower level of understanding. These theological trajectories notably developed outside of the university context at the level of popular devotion and traditional theological reflection, but the idea of monotheism also developed with the universities.

Monotheism in the Universities

During the seventeenth century there had been somewhat of a revolution in Indian philosophy, again in Bengal, with Nyāya philosophy, as Ganeri has shown. Ragunātha Śiromaṇi developed a new kind of thinking through traditional philosophical problems with a fresh logic (Ganeri 2014: 44–52). Thus, for example, epistemology was enhanced through the application of deductive logic. But although the earlier Nyāya tradition had articulated solid arguments for monotheism that were adopted by Śaiva theologians, as we have seen, the new Nyāya was not focused on the existence of God but on more worldly philosophical problems, such as what can be known and arguments around the nature of logic. With colonialism under the British, universities were established in the nineteenth century that became major centres of learning, studying subjects that included philosophy but not theology. Philosophy flourished in the university system during the twentieth century with centres of excellence, not only in Bengal, particularly Calcutta, but also in Mysore, Madras, Bombay, and Allahabad, 'the Oxford of the East', producing important philosophers such as K. C. Bhattacharya, M. Hiryanna, and Ankul Chandra Mukerji, although they are little studied in the West (Bhushan and Garfield 2016: 751). Mention should also be made of the first-rate historians of philosophy S. N. Dasgupta and Sarvepalli Radhakrishnan, future president of India, who held the first Spalding Chair in Eastern Religions and Ethics at All Souls College, Oxford.

Philosophy within the universities was influenced by Western philosophy but also by intellectual currents outside the university system, particularly the nineteenth-century Hindu Renaissance and the Neo-Vedanta of Vivekananda and his followers, who taught a form of non-dualism, as we have seen. Apart from Vivekananda, the great poet Rabindranath Tagore was a strong influence and another Bengali, Aurobindo Ghosh, fused Hegelian philosophy with Advaita, although operating outside the mainstream university system in his ashram in Pondicherry. It would be hard to describe Aurobindo's neo-Hegelian emanationism as a monotheism, but he has been a significant intellectual presence and influence. Mohandas Gandhi, so important in India's independence, might be described as a monotheist, identifying God with truth. He wrote a commentary on the *Bhagavad-gītā*, as did his political rival Tilak from his prison cell in Mandalay. Although acknowledging the transcendence of God in the text, Tilak was more interested in the *Bhagavad-gītā*'s political message as a martial statement about a nation's self-assertion in the context of throwing off the colonial yoke. It is probably fair to say that monotheism was not an intellectual position high on the list of priorities of any of these thinkers. Indeed, the Advaita Vedānta revival stemming from Vivekananda, of which Aurobindo, Tagore, and others were a part, was decidedly not monotheistic in advocating a kind of idealism.

The discourse of an explicit monotheism has therefore largely developed outside of the university system. Apart from Kṛṣṇa worship in Bengal and its theological articulation by Bhaktivinod and his descendants, monotheism had not been a strategy for intellectual decolonization in India. One reason for this, of course, was the necessity of establishing India as a secular state with Gandhi and Nehru because of the potential for conflict between Islam, Hinduism, and Sikhism. Indeed, secularism for Nehru was an attempt to secure human rights in the new democratic state, assuming a commitment to freedom of religion as well as to constitutional rights that neither mentioned religion nor opposed it (Bilgrami 2016: 706). While the appeal of Hindu monotheism is apparent at the popular level, and in the election of BJP governments who articulate a Hindu voice, Hindu monotheism remains largely devotional rather than intellectual. Many Hindus will regard themselves as monotheists who worship one God through different forms; the many Hindu gods are articulations of a transcendent deity. This is probably the general position of well-educated, anglophone Hindus in India and in the Hindu diaspora, although polytheism still holds sway at popular social levels, articulated only in vernacular languages.

Because of theology's exclusion from the secular university system, a rigorous intellectual monotheism comparable to Christian theology in Western universities has not developed in the Indian university system. Philosophy has turned to indigenous philosophies, particularly Advaita Vedānta, but on the whole has paid little attention to monotheism. Indeed, secular, postcolonial critique has been the order of the day in many philosophy departments, which have tended to veer away from theological discourse, regarding theology as part of a colonial imposition. Lastly in this short survey we need to mention that giant in Indian philosophy, Kṛṣṇa Chandra Bhattacharya (1875–1949). Colonialism is not only overt but subtle and has exercised a dominating influence on India such that Indian modes of thinking have been occluded. Bhattacharya drew on both Western philosophy, such as Kant's idea of freedom, and Advaita Vedānta's idea of the witnessing consciousness to produce a critical philosophy rooted in Indian tradition, although some philosophers have rejected this idea on the grounds that philosophy operates outside the boundaries of tradition (Ganeri 2016: 718–36).

Comparative Theology

Through the twentieth century and into the twenty-first there have been Hindu intellectuals, and Hindu monotheism has been brought into dialogue with Western monotheisms, particularly Christianity, because that was the religion of the colonizers, even though Syriac Christianity has been in Indian since around the seventh century. In some ways, because of the duration of its presence in the subcontinent, Christianity might be said to be an Indic tradition – it is much older, for example, than Gauḍīya Vaiṣṇavism. Theological dialogue between Hinduism and Christianity has become an important theme in intellectual discourse with Christian and Hindu theologians beginning to constructively engage with each other's thinking. One thinks of Rowland Williams at Lampeter, who wrote a book as an imaginary dialogue between a Christian and a Hindu theologian in the mid-nineteenth century (Williams 1856), and for all criticism that can be levelled against them, the Theosophists privileged Hindu thinking, especially Advaita, over Western thought. The Jesuits in particular have had a long engagement with Hindu thinking since Roberto de Nobili (1579–1656) through to the Indian Jesuit study of Hinduism by Mariasursai Dhavamony (1925–2014) (Clooney 2017: 29–40), and many thinkers have embarked on the serious study of Hindu theology, such as Swami Abhishiktananda, Raimon Panikkar, Eric Lott, Julius Lipner, and Francis Clooney. There has also been Hindu engagement with Christianity, such as with Brahmabandhab Upadhay (1861–1907), who became a Catholic convert (Lipner 1999). Clooney draws our attention also to a number of Indian scholars writing in English doing comparative work from a Hindu perspective with a view to finding common ground between religions and philosophies. Algondavilli Govindacharya (*c.* 1860–1940) is one such scholar; a Śrī Vaiṣṇava in the tradition of Rāmānuja, he articulated the idea of wisdom stemming from revelation. Others include comparative philosopher Brajendranath Seal (1864–1938), Kotta Satchidananda Murty (1924–2011), Daya Kṛṣṇa (1924–2007), Arvind Sharma, and Anantanand Rambachan. Clooney also discusses the holders of the Spalding Professorship of Eastern Religion and Ethics, Sarvepalli Radhakrishnan (1888–1975), R. C. Zaehner (1913–74), and B. K. Matilal (1935–91). Clooney's detailed scholarship on Hindu and Christian monotheism and the development of comparative theology has done much to bring Hindu monotheism on to the intellectual agenda in the contemporary anglophone world, although Lipner has raised engaging concerns about issues raised by such an enterprise, such as whether there is a need for the ideological stance of the scholar to be revealed, how we inquire into the nature of truth in a comparative theological manner, and what kinds of virtues are needed in such an inquiry (Lipner 2019) .

While the study of the philological and text-historical dimensions of Hindu monotheisms has developed with a high degree of precision – particularly of the Śaiva traditions in centres of learning such as the Centre d'Indologie in Pondicherry – philosophical and theological inquiry with a matching degree of philosophical precision, such as identified by Lipner, has been slower to develop. The text-historical study of Bengali Vaiṣṇavism has grown in recent years (e.g. Stewart 2010) and here there is more philosophical and theological investment in examining not only the sources but in treating Vaiṣṇavism as a living tradition that can develop intellectually in a global context through engagement with contemporary thinking, including dialogue with other religions (Wong 2015: 323). Indeed, important to note in this regard is the Swami Narayan tradition, a form of Hinduism that has become dominant especially in the West, keen to engage theologically with Western theologians and to promote an intellectually rigorous Hindu monotheism (Paramtattvadas 2017: 3–5). A cosmopolitan intellectual trajectory for Hindu monotheism needs to develop to ensure the global relevance of this discourse. If Theology as an academic discipline is to remain in secular universities, then it will inevitably be transformed through its engagement with other theologies, and Hindu monotheism may be part of that transformation.

References

Assmann, Jan. (2008). *Of God and Gods: Egypt and the Rise of Monotheism*. Madison: University of Wisconsin Press.

Bartley, Christopher. (2002). *The Theology of Rāmānuja: Realism and Religion*. London: Curzon Press.

Bellah, Robert N. and Hans Joas (eds.). (2012). *The Axial Age and Its Consequences*. Cambridge, MA: Belknap Press.

Bhatta, Jayanta. (1969). *Nyāya-mañjarī*, edited by Vidvan K. S. Varadacarya. Mysore: Oriental Research Institute.

Bhatta, Jayanta. (1978). *Nyāya-mañjarī*, translated by J. V. Bhattacharyya. Delhi: Motilal Banarsidass.

Bhaṭṭa, Jayanta. (2005). *Much Ado About Religion*, translated by Csaba Dezso. Clay Sanskrit Library. New York: New York University Press.

Bhattacharyya, Gopikamohan. (1961). *Studies in Nyāya-Vaiśeṣika Theism*. Calcutta: Sanskrit College.

Bhushan, Nalini and Jay L. Garfield. (2016). 'Ankul Chandra Mukerji: The Modern Subject', in Jonardon Ganeri (ed.), *The Oxford Handbook of Indian Philosophy*. Oxford: Oxford University Press, pp. 750–65.

Bilgrami, Akeel. 2016. 'Nehru, Gandhi, and Contexts of Indian Secularism', in Jonardon Ganeri (ed.), *The Oxford Handbook of Indian Philosophy*. Oxford: Oxford University Press, pp. 693–717.

Bilimoria, P. 1990. 'Hindu Doubts about God: Toward a Mīmāmsā Deconstruction', *International Philosophical Quarterly*, vol. 30, 481–99.

Bisschop, Peter. 2006. *Early Śaivism and the Skanda Purāṇa*. Leiden: Brill.

Bose, Mandakranta (ed.). 2018. *The Oxford History of Hinduism: The Goddess*. Oxford: Oxford University Press.

Bronkhorst, Johannes. 1996. 'God's Arrival in the Vaiṣeśika System', *Journal of Indian Philosophy*, vol. 24 (3), pp. 281–94.

Brown, M. 2008. 'The Design Argument in Classical Hindu Thought', *International Journal of Hindu Studies*, vol. 12 (2), 103–51.

Bryant, Edwin F. 2003. *Krishna, the Beautiful Legend of God (*Bhāgavata Purāṇa *Book X)*. London: Penguin.

Bryant, Edwin F. 2017. *Bhakti Yoga: Tales and Teachings from the* Bhāgavata Purāṇa. New York: North Point Press.

Bulcke, C. S. J. 1968. *The Theism of Nyāya-Vaiśeṣika: Its Origin and Early Development*. Delhi: Motilal Banarsidass.

Burton, A. P. 2000. Temples, Texts, and Taxes: The *Bhagavad-gītā* and the Politico-Religious Identity of the Caitanya Sect. PhD, Australian National University.

Busch, Alison. 2011. *Poetry of Kings: The Classical Hindi Literature of Mughal India*. Oxford: Oxford University Press.

Carman, John and Vasudha Narayan. 1989. *The Tamil Veda: Pillan's Interpretation of the* Tiruvaymoli. Chicago: University of Chicago Press.

Chakrabarti, K. K. 1975. 'The Nyāya-Vaiśeṣika Theory of Universals', *Journal of Indian Philosophy*, vol. 3, pp. 363–82.

Chemparathy, G. 1968–9. 'Two Early Buddhist Refutations of the Existence of the Īśvara as the Creator of the Universe', *Wiener Zeitschrift für die Kunde Süd- und Ostasiens und Archiv für indische Philosophie*, vol. 12–13, pp. 85–100.

Chemparathy, G. 1972. *An Indian Rational Theology: Introduction to Udayana's* Nyāyakusumañjali. Publications of the De Nobili Research Library, Vol. 1. Vienna: Gerold & Co.

Chettiarthodi, Rajendran. 2013. 'Sanskritization in Regional History: A Study in the Historiography of Atula's *Mūṣikavaṃśa*', *Cracow Indological Studies*, vol. 15, pp. 67–80.

Clooney, Francis, 2017. *The Future of Hindu-Christian Studies: A Theological Inquiry*. London: Routledge.

Cohen, Signe. 2008. *Text and Authority in the Older Upaniṣads*. Leiden: Brill.

Collet, S. D. 1962. *The Life and Letters of Raja Rammohan Roy*. Calcutta: Sadharan Brahmo Samaj.

Crawford, S. C. 1987. *Ram Mohan Roy: Social, Political and Religious Reform in Nineteenth Century India*. New York: Paragon House.

Dasgupta, Surendranath. 1975 (1922). *A History of Indian Philosophy*, 4 vols. Delhi: Motilal Banarsidass.

Dasti, Mathew R. and Edwin F. Bryant (eds.). 2014. *Free Will, Agency, and Selfhood in Indian Philosophy*. Oxford: Oxford University Press.

De Simini, Florinda. 2016. *Of Gods and Books: Ritual and Knowledge Transmission in the Manuscript Cultures of Premodern India*. Berlin: De Gruyter.

Dirks, Nicholas. 1988. *The Hollow Crown: Ethnohistory of an Indian Kingdom*. Cambridge: Cambridge University Press.

Dumont, Louis. 1980 (1970). *Homo Hierarchicus: The Caste System and Its Implications*, translated by Mark Sainsbury, Louis Dumont, and Basia Gulati. Chicago: Chicago University Press.

Dunn, B. P. 2016. *A. J. Appasamy and His Reading of Rāmānuja: A Comparative Study in Divine Embodiment*. Oxford: Oxford University Press.

Dyczkowski, Mark. 1990. *Self-Awareness, Own-Being, and Egoity*. Varanasi: Ratna Printing Works.

Elizarenkova, T. Y. 1995. *Language and Style of the Vedic Ṛṣis*. Albany: SUNY Press.

Fisher, Elaine M. 2017. *Hindu Pluralism: Religion and the Public Sphere in Early Modern South India*. Berkeley: University of California Press.

Fitzgerald, Timothy. 2000. *The Ideology of Religious Studies*. Oxford: Oxford University Press.

Flood, Gavin. 2019a. *Religion and the Philosophy of Life*. Oxford: Oxford University Press.

Flood, Gavin. 2019b. *Western Perspectives on Dialogue in a World of Conflict and Violence*. Interreligious Relations: Occasional Papers of The Studies in Interreligious Relations in Plural Societies Programme, Vol. 9. Singapore: Rajaratnam School of International Studies.

Flood, Gavin and Charles Martin. 2012. *The Bhagavad Gita: A New Translation*. New York: Norton.

Frazier, Jessica. 2008. *Reality, Religion, and Passion: Indian and Western Approaches in Hans Georg Gadamer and Rūpa Gosvāmi*. Lanham: Lexington.

Ganeri, Jonardon. 2014. *The Lost Age of Reason: Philosophy in Early Modern India 1450–1700*. Oxford: Oxford University Press.

Ganeri, Jonardon. 2016. 'Freedom in Thinking: The Immersive Cosmopolitanism of Krishnachandra Bhattacharya', in Jonardon Ganeri (ed.), *The Oxford Handbook of Indian Philosophy*. Oxford: Oxford University Press, pp. 718–36.

Goodall, Dominic. 2004. *The* Parākhyatantra*: A Scripture of the Śaiva Siddhānta*. Pondicherry: Institut Français de Pondichéry.

Goswami, Tamal Krishna. 2012. *A Living Theology of Krishna Bhakti: Essential Teachings of A. C. Bhaktivedanta Swami Prabhupada*, edited by Graham Schweig. Oxford: Oxford University Press.

Gupta, Ravi M. 2007. *The Caitanya Vaiṣṇava Vedānta of Jīva Gosvāmī: When Knowledge Meets Devotion*. London: Routledge.

Gupta, Ravi M. and Kenneth R. Valpey (eds.). 2013. *The* Bhagavata Purana*: Sacred Text and Living Tradition*. New York: Columbia University Press.

Hacker, Paul. 1995. 'Aspects of Neo-Hinduism', in Wilhelm Halbfass (ed.), *Philology and Confrontation: Paul Hacker on Traditional and Modern Vedanta*. Albany: SUNY Press, pp. 229–55.

Hardy, Friedhelm. 1983. *Viraha Bhakti: The Early History of Kṛṣṇa Devotion in South India*. Oxford: Oxford University Press.

Hatcher, Brian. 1999. *Eclecticism and Modern Hindu Discourse*. Oxford: Oxford University Press.

Hatcher, Brian. 2008. *Bourgeois Hinduism or Faith of the Modern Vedantists: Rare Discourses from Early Colonial Bengal*. Oxford: Oxford University Press.

Hayes, R. 1988. 'Principled Atheism in the Buddhist Scholastic Tradition', *Journal of Indian Philosophy*, vol. 16, pp. 5–28.

Hedley, R. Douglas. 2016. *The Iconic Imagination*. London: Bloomsbury.

Heesterman, J. 1993. *The Broken World of Sacrifice: Essays in Ancient Indian Ritual*. Chicago: University of Chicago Press.

Hopkins, Steven P. 2007. *An Ornament for Jewels: Love Poems for the Lord of Gods, by Ventakesa*. Oxford: Oxford University Press.

Horstmann, Monika. 2009. *Der Zusammenhalt der Welt: Religiöse Herrschaftslegitimation und Religionspolitik Mahārāja Savāī Jaisinghs (1700–1743)*. Wiesbaden: Otto Harrassowitz.

Horstmann, Monika. 2012. 'Theology and Statecraft', in Rosalind O'Hanlon and David Washbrook (eds.), *Religious Cultures in Early Modern India: New Perspectives*. London: Routledge ch 3.

Horstmann, Monika. 2013. *Jaipur 1778: The Making of a King*. Weisbaden: Harrassowitz.

Hunt-Overzee, Anne. 1992. *The Body Divine: The Symbol of the Body in the Works of Teilhard de Chardin and Rāmānuja*. Cambridge: Cambridge University Press.

Inden, Ronald B. 1990. *Imagining India*. Cambridge, MA: Blackwell.

Jackson, R. 1986. 'Dharmakirit's Refutation of Theism', *Philosophy East and West*, vol. 36 (4), pp. 315–48.

Jamieson, Stephanie and Joel Brereton. 2017. 'Introduction', in *The Rig Veda* Vol. 1. Oxford: Oxford University Press. pp. 1–84.

Ježić, Mislav. 2009. 'The Triṣṭubh Hymn in the Bhagavadgītā', in Petteri Koskikallio (ed.), *Parallels and Comparisons*. Proceedings of the Fourth Dubrovnik International Conference on the Sanskrit Epics and Purāṇas, September 2005. Zagreb: Croatian Academy of Sciences and Arts, pp. 31–66.

Ježić, Mislav. 2021. 'The *Bhagavadgītā*: Indian Commentaries, Western Reception, and the History of Research', in Gavin Flood (ed.), *The Blackwell Companion to Hinduism*, 2nd ed. Oxford: Blackwell.

Juergensmeyer, Mark. 1991. *Radhasoami Reality: The Logic of a Modern Faith*. Princeton: Princeton University Press.

Kajiyama, Y. 1998. *An introduction to Buddhist Philosophy: An Annotated Translation of the Tarkabhāsā of Moksākaragupta*. Vienna: Arbeitskreis für Tibetische und Buddhistische Studien Universität Wien.

Kapila, Shruti and Faisal Devji (eds.). 2013. *Political Thought in Action: The* Bhagavad Gita *and Modern India*. Cambridge: Cambridge University Press.

Killingley, Dermot. 1993. *Rammohun Roy in Hindu and Christian Tradition: The Teape Lectures 1990*. Newcastle upon Tyne: Grevatt and Grevatt.

Kitcher, P. 2001. 'Real Realism: The Galilean Strategy', *Philosophical Review*, vol. 110, pp. 151–97.

Kulke, H. and D. Rothermund. 1998. *History of India*. London: Routledge.

Leinhard, Siegfried. 1984. *A History of Classical Poetry: Sanskrit, Pali, Prakrit*. Weisbaden: Otto Harrassowitz.

Lévi, Sylvain. 1898. *La Doctrine de sacrifice dans les Brahmanas*. Paris: Ernest Leroux.

Lipner, Julius. 1978. 'The Christian and Vedāntic Theories of Originative Causality: A Study in Transcendence', *Philosophy East and West*, vol. 28, pp. 53–68.

Lipner, Julius. 1984. 'The World as God's "Body": In Pursuit of Dialogue with Rāmānuja',*Religious Studies*, vol. 20, pp. 145–61.

Lipner, Julius. 1999. *Brahmabandhab Upadhyay: The Life and Thought of a Revolutionary*. Delhi: Oxford University Press.

Lipner, Julius. 2017. *Hindu Images and Their Worship with Special Reference to Vaiṣṇavism: A Philosophical-Theological Inquiry*. London: Routledge.

Lipner, Julius. 2019. *Comparative Theology in the Academic Study of Religion: An Inquiry*. Interreligious Relations: Occasional Papers of the Studies in Interreligious Relations in Plural Societies Programme, Vol. 6.Singapore: Rajaratnam School of International Studies.

Lovejoy, Arthur O. 1936. *The Great Chain of Being*. Harvard: Harvard University Press.

Macnicol, Nicol. 1915. *Indian Theism from the Vedic to the Muhammadan Period*. London: Oxford University Press.

Malinar, Angelika. 2007. *The* Bhagavad Gita*: Doctrines and Contexts*. Cambridge: Cambridge University Press.

Manzaridis, Georgios. 'Simplicity of God According to St Gregory Palamas', in Constantinos Athanasopoulos (ed.), *Triune God: Incomprehensible Knowable – The Philosophical and Theological Significance of St Gregory Palamas for Contemporary Philosophy and Theology*. Newcastle upon Tyne: Cambridge Scholars Press, pp. 19–27.

Marriot, McKim. 1976. 'Hindu Transactions: Diversity without Dualism', in Bruce Kapferer (ed.), *Transaction and Meaning: Directions in the Anthropology of Exchange and Symbolic Behaviour*. Philadelphia: Institute for the Study of Human Issues, pp. 109–42.

Michaels, Axel. 2016. *Homo Ritualis: Hindu Ritual and its Significance for Ritual Theory*. Oxford: Oxford University Press.

Minkowski, Christopher Z. and Polly O'Hanlon (eds.). 2015. *Scholar Intellectuals in Early Modern India: Discipline, Sect, Lineage and Community*. London: Taylor and Francis.

Modi, P. M. 1932. *Akṣara: A Forgotten Chapter in the History of Indian Philosophy*. Baroda: State Press.

Moise, Ionut. 2017. The Nature and Function of Vaiśeṣika Soteriology with Particular Reference to Candrānanda's Vṛtti. DPhil, Oxford University.

Müller, Max. 1899. *The Six Systems of Indian Philosophy*. London: Longmans, Green, and Co.

Nicholson, Andrew J. 2010. *Unifying Hinduism: Philosophy and Identity in Indian Intellectual History*. New York: Columbia University Press.

Novetzske, Christian Lee. 2011. *Religion and Public Memory: A Cultural History of Saint Namdev in India*. New York: Columbia University Press.

Oberlies, Thomas. 1995. 'Die Śvetāśvatara Upaniṣad: Einleitung-Edition und Übersetzung von Adhyāya I', *Wiener Zeitschrift für die Kunde Sudasiens*, vol. 39, pp. 61–102.

Oberlies, Thomas. 1998. 'Die Śvetāśvatara Upaniṣad: Edition und Übersetzung von Adhyāya IV–VI (Studien zu den "mittleren" Upaniṣads II – 3. Teil)', *Wiener Zeitschrift für die Kunde Südasiens*, vol. 42, pp. 77–138.

O'Connell, Joseph. 2019. *Caitanya Vaiṣṇavism in Bengal: Social Impact and Historical Implications*, edited by Rembert Lutjeharms London: Routledge.

O'Hanlon, Rosalind and David Washbrook (eds.). 2012. *Religious Cultures in Early Modern India: New Perspectives*. London: Routledge London

Okita, Kiyokazu. 2014. *Hindu Theology in Early Modern South Asia: The Rise of Devotionalism and the Politics of Genealogy*. Oxford: Oxford University Press.

Olivelle, Patrick. 1998. *The Early Upaniṣads*. Oxford: Oxford University Press.

Olivelle, Patrick and Timothy Lubin (eds.). 2017. *Hindu Law*. Oxford: Oxford University Press.

Padoux, André. 2003. 'Mantra', in Gavin Flood (ed.), *The Blackwell Companion to Hinduism*. Oxford: Blackwell, pp. 478–92.

Paramtattvadas, Swami. 2017. *An Introduction to Swaminarayan Hindu Theology*. Cambridge: Cambridge University Press.

Paranjape, Makarand P. 2015. *Swami Vivekananda: A Contemporary Reader*. London: Routledge.

Patel, Sunit. 2018. Politics and Religion in Eighteenth-Century North India: The Rise of Public Theology in Gauḍīya Vaiṣṇavism. DPhil, University of Oxford.

Patil, P. 2009. *Against a Hindu God: Buddhist Philosophy of Religion in India*. New York: Columbia University Press.

Pauwels, Heidi. 2009. *The Goddess as Role Model: Sita and Radha in Scripture and on Screen*. Oxford: Oxford University Press.

Peabody, Norbert. 2003. *Hindu Kingship and Polity in Pre-Colonial India*. Cambridge: Cambridge University Press.

Phillips, S. 1995. *Classical Indian Metaphysics: Refutations of Realism and the Emergence of 'New Logic'*. Chicago: Open Court.

Pollock, Sheldon. 2006. *The Language of the Gods in the World of Men: Sanskrit, Culture and Power in Premodern India*. Berkeley: University of California Press.

Rāmānuja. 1953. *Vedāntasāra*, translated and edited by V. Krishnamacharya and M. B. Narasimha Ayyangar. Madras: Adyar Library.

Ramanujan, A. K. 1973. *Speaking of Śiva*. London: Penguin.

Ram-Prasad, C. 2013. *Divine Self, Human Self*. London: Bloomsbury.

Ratié, Isabelle. 2011. *Le Soi et l'Autre: Identité, difference et altérité dand la philosophie de a Pratyabhijñā*. Leiden: Brill.

Ratié, Isabelle. 2016. 'Utpaladeva's Proof of God: On the Purpose of the *Īśvarasiddhi*', in Raffaele Torella and Bettina Bäumer (eds), *Utpaladeva: Philosopher of Recognition*. Shimla: Indian Institute of Advanced Study, pp. 257–340.

Sanderson, Alexis. 1988. 'The Tantric and Śaiva Traditions', in Stuart Sutherland, Leslie Houlden, and Friedhelm Hardy (eds.), *The World's Religions*. London: Routledge, pp. 660–704.

Sanderson, Alexis. 2009. 'The Śaiva Age', in Shingo Einoo (ed.), *Development and Genesis of Tantrism*. Tokyo: Institute of Oriental Culture, pp. 41–149.

Sanderson, Alexis. 2019. 'How Public Was Śaivism?', in Nina Mirnig, Marion Rastelli, and Vincent Eltschinger (eds.), *Tantric Communities in Context*. Vienna: Austrian Academy of Sciences Press, pp. 19–65.

Sardella, Ferdinando. 2013. *Modern Hindu Personalism: The History, Life, and Thought of Bhaktisiddhanta Sarasvati*. Oxford: Oxford University Press.

Sarma, Deepak. 2003. *An Introduction to Mādhva Vedānta*. Aldershot: Ashgate.

Schmidt, Charlotte. 2010. *Le Don de voir: première representations krishnaïtes de la region de Mathurā*. Paris: École Française d'Extrême-Orient.

Schouten, Jan Peter. 1995. *Revolution of the Mystics: On the Social Aspects of Vīraśaivism*. Delhi: MLBD.

Schrader, Otto. 1916. *An Introduction to the Pañcarātra and the Ahirbudhnya Saṃhitā*. Madras: Adyar Library.

Siegel, Lee. 1978. *Sacred and Profane Dimensions of Love in Indian Traditions as Exemplified in The Gītagovinda of Jayadeva*. Oxford: Oxford University Press.

Staal, Frits. 1989. *Rules without Meaning: Ritual, Mantras and the Human Sciences*. New York: Peter Lang.

Stein, Burton. 1989. *The New Cambridge History of India – Vijayanagara*. Cambridge: Cambridge University Press.

Stewart, Tony. 2010. *The Final Word: The* Caitanya Caritāmṛta *and the Grammar of Religious Tradition*. Oxford: Oxford University Press.

Stoker, Valerie. 2016. *Polemics and Patronage in the City of Victory: Vyāsatīrtha, Hindu Sectarianism, and the Sixteenth-Century Vijayanagara Court*. Oakland: University of California Press.

Taylor, Charles. 2004. *Modern Social Imaginaries*. Durham, NC: Duke University Press.

Taylor, Charles. 2007. *The Secular Age*. Cambridge, MA: Belknap Press of Harvard University Press.

Thieme, Paul. 1965. 'Īśopaniṣad (= Vājasaneyi-Saṃhitā 40) 1–14', *Journal of the American Oriental Society*, vol. 85, pp. 89–99.

Timalsina, Sthaneshwar. 2015. *Language of Images: Visualization and Meaning in Tantras*. New York: Peter Lang.

Torella, Raffaele. 2016. 'Introduction', in Raffaele Torella and Bettina Bäumer (eds), *Utpaladeva: Philosopher of Recognition*. Shimla: Indian Institute of Advanced Study, pp. 1–13.

Turner, Denys. 2002. *How to Be an Atheist: Inaugural Lecture Delivered at the University of Cambridge*. Cambridge: Cambridge University Press.

Turner, Denys. 2004. *Faith, Reason and the Existence of God*. Cambridge University Press.

Vattanky, G.S.J. 1984. *Gaṅgeśa's Philosophy of God*. Madras: The Adyar Library and Research Centre.

Watson, Alex, Dominic Goodall, and S. L. P. Anjaneya Sarma. 2013. *An Inquiry into the Nature of Liberation: Bhaṭṭa Rāmakaṇṭha's* Paramokṣanirāsakārikāvṛtti. *A Commentary on Sadyojyotiḥ's Refutation of Twenty Conceptions of the Liberated State (Mokṣa)*. Pondicherry: Institut Français de Pondichéry.

Williams, Rowan. 2012. *Faith in the Public Square*. London: Bloomsbury.

Williams, Rowland. 1856. *Parmeswara-jnyana-goshthi: A Dialogue of the Knowledge of the Supreme Lord, in which are compared the claims of Christianity and Hinduism, and various questions of Indian Religion and Literature fairly discussed*. Cambridge: Deighton, Bell and Co.

Wong, Lucian. 2015. 'Gauḍīya Vaiṣṇava Studies: Mapping the Field', *Religions of South Asia*, vol. 9 (3), pp. 305–31.

Wong, Lucian. 2018. 'Universalising Inclusivism – and Its Limits: Bhaktivinod and the Experiential Turn', *Journal of South Asian Intellectual History*, vol. 1 (2), pp. 1–43.

Zaehner, R. C. 1966. *The* Bhagavad Gita. Oxford: Oxford University Press.

Acknowledgements

I would like to thank the editors of the Elements series, Chad Meister and Paul Moser, for inviting me to write on this topic and to conversations with a number of people about it, particularly with my wife Dr Kwankui Leung who, as always, made significant observations, to friends and colleagues at the Oxford Centre for Hindu Studies (Dr Jessica Frazier, Shaunaka Rishi Das, Dr Rembert Lutjeharms, Dr Bjarne Wernicke-Olesen, and Lucian Wong), to my friends and colleagues Professor Julius Lipner and Professor Frank Clooney SJ, and to friends at Campion Hall, particularly the Master Nick Austin SJ, the Assistant Master Pat Riordan SJ, and the Past Master James Hanvey SJ. In ways unbeknownst to them they have all contributed. I would like to dedicate this book to Shaunaka Rishi Das.

Professor Gavin Flood FBA,
Oxford, Autumn 2019

Cambridge Elements ☰

Religion and Monotheism

Paul K. Moser

Loyola University Chicago

Paul K. Moser is Professor of Philosophy at Loyola University Chicago. He is the author of *The God Relationship; The Elusive God* (winner of national book award from the Jesuit Honor Society)*; The Evidence for God; The Severity of God; Knowledge and Evidence (*all Cambridge University Press); and *Philosophy after Objectivity* (Oxford University Press); co-author of *Theory of Knowledge* (Oxford University Press); editor of *Jesus and Philosophy* (Cambridge University Press) and *The Oxford Handbook of Epistemology* (Oxford University Press); co-editor of *The Wisdom of the Christian Faith (*Cambridge University Press). He is the co-editor with Chad Meister of the book series *Cambridge Studies in Religion, Philosophy, and Society.*

Chad Meister

Bethel University

Chad Meister is Professor of Philosophy and Theology and Department Chair at Bethel College. He is the author of *Introducing Philosophy of Religion* (Routledge, 2009), *Christian Thought: A Historical Introduction*, 2nd edition (Routledge, 2017), and *Evil: A Guide for the Perplexed*, 2nd edition (Bloomsbury, 2018). He has edited or co-edited the following: *The Oxford Handbook of Religious Diversity* (Oxford University Press, 2010), *Debating Christian Theism* (Oxford University Press, 2011), with Paul Moser, *The Cambridge Companion to the Problem of Evil* (Cambridge University Press, 2017), and with Charles Taliaferro, *The History of Evil* (Routledge 2018, in six volumes).

About the Series

This Cambridge Element series publishes original concise volumes on monotheism and its significance. Monotheism as occupied inquirers since the time of the Biblical patriarch, and it continues to attract interdisciplinary academic work today. Engaging, current, and concise, the Elements benefit teachers, researched, and advanced students in religious studies, Biblical studies, theology, philosophy of religion, and related fields.

Cambridge Elements

Religion and Monotheism

Elements in the Series

Buddhism and Monotheism
Peter Harvey

Monotheism and the Meaning of Life
T.J. Mawson

Monotheism and Contemporary Atheism
Michael Ruse

Monotheism and Hope in God
William J. Wainwright

Monotheism and Religious Diversity
Roger Trigg

Divine Ideas
Thomas M. Ward

Hindu Monotheism
Gavin Flood

A full series listing is available at: www.cambridge.org/er&m

www.ingramcontent.com/pod-product-compliance
Ingram Content Group UK Ltd.
Pitfield, Milton Keynes, MK11 3LW, UK
UKHW020455010325
455719UK00016B/589

9 781108 731140